WE COOK FILIPINO

Heart-Healthy Recipes and Inspiring Stories from 36 Filipino Food Personalities and Award-Winning Chefs

Compiled and edited by
Jacqueline Chio–Lauri

TUTTLE Publishing

Tokyo | Rutland, Vermont | Singapore

Contents

CHAPTER 1
Kanin at Agahan
Rice and Morning Meals

CHAPTER 2
Baon Packed Lunches

CHAPTER 3
Pulutan, Sabaw at Merienda
Nibbles, Soups and Noshes

Kumain Ka Na? Have You Eaten?

This is not a traditional cookbook: it's a collection of stories and recipes from Filipino chefs, food writers and influencers across the globe. You'll enjoy reading the tales the contributors have to tell as much as you'll enjoy preparing the delicious recipes they share. Also, all the recipes in this book are "heart healthy." They comply with specific recommendations by the American Heart Association and with general recommendations taken from the *Dietary Guidelines for Americans* issued by the US Department of Health. This book is for those of you who want to savor life as much as you want to savor Filipino food, in all its healthful, tasteful and heartful goodness.

Kumain ka na? There is no expression that gives a better glimpse into Filipino food culture than this question, which means "Have you eaten?" It's a common greeting Filipinos use, and is almost interchangeable with "Kumusta?" (How are you?). On the surface, it asks, "Have you eaten?" Beneath the surface it means, "I care." The instinct to care for others — even strangers, is strong in Filipino culture, and the urge to feed and nourish is second nature.

Digging deeper, the question unravels a Filipino belief that food is the primary determinant of a person's state of well-being — without having eaten, all else is of less consequence. Our need for food — to satisfy our stomach, palate, mind, heart or soul — shapes our cuisine. In this book, this need, and the way we fulfill it, is reflected in the stories and recipes of thirty-six men and women of Filipino heritage, all diasporic trailblazers, many of them well-known chefs.

They include James Beard Award qualifiers Paolo Mendoza, Margarita Manzke, Carlo Lamagna and Amormia Orino, who share with us not just their own spin on beloved recipes, including the renowned adobo, the street fare tokneneng and the classic ginataan, but also their personal stories about what food means to them. Chef Margarita discovers that the secret to a great life is no different from the secret to a great adobo; culture shock turns into a delicious adventure when Carlo moves back to the Philippines; Amormia shares her heart-wrenching but hopeful story about her aging mother, the passionate cook of the family.

The brief I gave the contributors was that the stories and their associated recipes had to be "from the heart," as well as good for the heart. I asked them to write about what makes them happy, despite their own personal conflicts, as I know from my own battles with an anxiety disorder that fear, resentment and stress can be as harmful to our hearts as excessive salt, sugar and fat. The result is a cookbook that presents food as something as central to our well-being, as the common Filipino greeting implies, with a focus on recipes using ingredients and cooking methods that are literally good for our physical health.

Ultimately, we share our stories and recipes in this book, because we care and because we cook! And so, we ask you, "Kumain ka na?" Let us nourish your body and your soul as you give your palate and your heart a treat.

I sincerely hope you enjoy reading our stories and find value in our recipes. It would mean the world to me if you could write a review at your online store, book site or on social media — even just a sentence or two.

This book took four years from its inception to its birth. I gave it my all because I believe that it can serve my community and yours — communities that are at risk of heart disease. If you think that this collection could inspire someone to be happier and healthier, a review from you could go a long way toward helping other readers find this book.

Maraming salamat po!
— Jacqueline Chio-Lauri
Editor and Compiler

Filipino Food: An Evolution

The sixteenth-century Magellan expedition, fueled by a hunger for food, was led by Portuguese explorer Ferdinand Magellan and was the first voyage around the world. The fleet reached the Philippines in 1521. Before this, Filipino foods were the gift of nature's bounty — either cooked on an open fire, grilled over coal, baked in a pit, boiled or simmered in a clay pot, cooked wrapped in leaves or in bamboo culms under or above fire, or simply marinated to preserve it.

Though precolonial fare bore resemblance to the food of the islands' early Austronesian settlers, it had traces of the cuisines of south Asian, Arab, and Chinese trading partners. Filipino cultural historian and food writer Doreen Fernandez characterized the emerging cuisine in that period as clearly showing original flavors. One of those flavors was described as "very much salted" by Antonio Pigafetta, the Italian explorer and chronicler of the Magellan expedition.

Clearly, the use of salt was already widespread across the Philippines when Magellan's fleet arrived. In the hot climes, with temperatures permanently in the danger zone range, salting food was an important preservation method. Generous helpings of unsalted rice tamed the excessive saltiness of other dishes, forming an indispensable coupling of salty fare with indulgent servings of the staple grain.

Aside from saltiness, Filipinos developed a discernible preference for sweetness, not only in desserts, but in practically everything. This dates back to precolonial times, when mothers gave their babies sugarcane as pacifiers. Children ate sugarcane mixed with rice, while adults chewed it to stave off hunger and give themselves a quick energy boost. While sugarcane was grown archipelago-wide, the know-how to process it into sugar only emerged during Spanish rule (1565–1898). Originally sugar was reserved for the aristocracy, but by the mid-1700s, the Philippines was manufacturing enough sugar to keep up with local demand with a bit to spare for export. As sugar became a

cheap commodity, it was used as preservative, as a mitigator of saltiness, as an accessible source of energy, as a way of stanching hunger, and as an in-between-meals treat.

Traditionally, meals consisted of rice and fish, or vegetables enhanced with bits of fish and meat. Meat, especially pork, was a luxury reserved for special occasions—until the spread of Christianity. By eating pork, Catholics set themselves apart from rival religions that prohibited it, namely Islam and Judaism.

Native Filipinos, exposed to the food of their colonizers, learned to adapt Spanish dishes to their taste using local ingredients until they became their own. This is the origin of dishes such as longanisa, torta and relleno. Adapting and adopting foreign dishes, serves to fulfill a variety of needs, including those of the colonized to copy the colonizers to be like one of them, while maintaining the longing to stay true to one's identity.

The process of adapting and adopting continued under the period of American conquest from 1899 to 1946 and is reflected in dishes such as fried chicken, ice candy and sorbetes. Institutionalized food safety, imported shelf-stable highly processed foods or canned goods like Spam, sweetened condensed milk,

and fruit cocktail in syrup, were introduced and assimilated into Filipino kitchens. New methods of food preservation and preparation met the needs of modern living.

Rapid urbanization in the years that followed saw a decline in the traditional self-sufficient home, such as the bahay kubo (cubed hut) with vegetable patches and fruit trees. A culture of instant gratification, of increasing numbers of women in the workforce and of long commutes saw Filipinos eating fewer home-cooked meals, more fast food, and eating out more frequently.

Spurred by the search for a better life, millions of Filipinos migrated and continue to migrate to the United States, Europe and other parts of the world. As the needs of Filipinos under their colonizers led to Western dishes recreated with a Filipino twist, migration has led to Filipino dishes recreated with a Western twist. The longing of migrant Filipinos to keep their food culture alive often means substituting ingredients with locally accessible produce and adjusting methods of cooking to fit new lifestyles. This evolution can be seen in our recipes, such as pinakbet, adobo, tinola, atchara, kare-kare and turon—all of which you can find in this book.

What Are "Heart-Healthy" Recipes?

According to the World Health Organization, cardiovascular disease (CVD) is the leading cause of death globally, claiming an estimated 17.9 million lives each year. To put this into context, Covid-19 took about 2.2 million lives worldwide in a year. Many of these deaths were of those who had pre-existing heart or hypertensive conditions — which are prevalent in Filipino communities[1]. However deadly, CVDs are preventable, even if we have genetic risk factors (researchers found that genes accounted for well under 7 percent of people's lifespan, which means over 93 percent of our health and longevity is in our own hands). Healthy eating is crucial, and I see Filipino food rising to the challenge without losing its core balance of tastes.

Though there is barely consensus among medical professionals about the best foods to eat, the recipes in this book align with the calorie, sodium and added sugar recommendations of the Heart-Check Recipe Certification Program guide published in May 2019 by the American Heart Association (AHA). They follow the AHA's recommendation of avoiding deep-frying and the use of bacon, butter, lard, ghee, margarine and MSG.

The recipes also follow the general recommendations of the *Dietary Guidelines for Americans* (DGA) 2020–2025 to decrease our intake of foods higher in sodium and added sugar, and increase our intake of nutrient-dense foods, such as vegetables, legumes, fruits and whole grains. The DGA suggests limiting saturated fat to less than 10 percent of the total calories you eat and drink each day. Though the effects to our health of different kinds of saturated fats are still contestable, I have included saturated fat values in the nutrition data of each recipe to help you plan your daily meals accordingly.

Last but not least, our recipes heed the universal rule that *eating should be pleasurable*!

[1] Coronado G, Chio-Lauri J, Cruz RD, Roman YM. Health Disparities of Cardiometabolic Disorders Among Filipino Americans: Implications for Health Equity and Community-Based Genetic Research. J Racial Ethn Health Disparities. 2022 Dec;9(6):2560-2567. doi: 10.1007/s40615-021-01190-6. Epub 2021 Nov 26. PMID: 34837163; PMCID: PMC9248953.

Glossary of Filipino Ingredients and Their Health Benefits

Cities with a large Filipino diaspora have Filipino supermarkets or grocers where the ingredients in this book can be found. Alternatively, Filipino ingredients are available in Asian grocery stores and can sometimes be found in the international or Asian food aisles of supermarkets. When buying packaged foods, make it a habit to check and compare salt, sugar and saturated fat content on nutrition labels.

 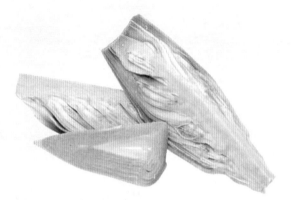

Annatto or achuete/atsuete seeds, the Philippines' natural food coloring, impart a desirable orangey tinge to dishes. Annatto, a native fruit of Mexico, was brought to the country by trading ships during the Spanish colonial era. Aside from Asian and Latin markets, well-stocked supermarkets may carry annatto seeds in their spice or international sections.

Bagoong guisado shrimp paste is available in jars. The sodium content of a tablespoon of bagoong guisado is about 540 mg (23 percent of our daily limit), depending on the brand, so check the nutritional information on the label.

Banana Saba banana is a native Philippine banana. Its health benefits are maximized if eaten raw, but it is used mainly for cooking: as a vegetable when unripe; as a fruit when ripe. It is high in starch and similar to potato in carbohydrate content. Bananas are a good source of potassium, which flushes sodium from our system.

Banana blossom/heart (puso ng saging) can be purchased fresh, but is more commonly found in cans in health food stores, Asian food shops or online. It looks and tastes more like an artichoke than a banana. It's a potent source of essential nutrients and antioxidants that help prevent heart disease.

Banana leaves (dahon ng saging) are not edible. In Filipino cooking, they are used to wrap food, to impart aroma and flavor. Wrapping fish in a banana leaf when cooking also keeps it from drying out. They are usually available frozen.

Bihon rice noodles are thin, dried rice noodles that are also available in regular supermarkets as rice vermicelli.

Bitter melon (ampalaya) is a vegetable known for its bitter taste and health benefits. This wrinkly gourd is preferably eaten while it's young and green, just before it yellows, because it becomes more bitter when it ripens. It contains dietary fiber, notable for potentially improving heart health.

Calamansi is a citrus fruit native to the Philippines, similar to lime but smaller in size. It's a good source of Vitamin C, an essential vitamin and antioxidant for relaxing the blood vessels that carry blood from the heart. You can also find bottled calamansi juice or puree in Filipino or Asian markets.

Cane vinegar (sukang Iloco/sukang maasim) is fermented sugar cane syrup.

Cassava (kamoteng kahoy) is also known as manioc or yuca. This high-calorie starchy root vegetable is sold ready grated and frozen in packs. It is rich in potassium, which may help lower blood pressure.

Chayote (sayote) is a squash with a similar texture and flavor profile to green papaya, and the two are interchangeable in Philippine cooking. Sayote contains a slew of healthy nutrients, including an antioxidant that lowers cholesterol. It also contains fiber, which is associated with lowering the risk of heart disease.

Coconuts are widely available fresh and husked in many supermarkets. They are rich in manganese, a nutrient essential to many bodily functions, including the metabolism of cholesterol.

Coconut cream (kakang gata) is a more concentrated and richer coconut milk. It usually comes from the first extract. You can find it in cans or cartons in supermarkets.

Coconut milk (gata) is the milky white liquid expressed from shredded coconut meat and water. Also available in cans or packs in powder form in supermarkets. Reduced fat or light coconut milk in cans are also available.

Coconut sap vinegar (sukang tuba) is unpasteurized and contains the natural mother, the cloudy film of sediment that settles at the bottom of the bottle. According to the Philippine Coconut Authority, coconut vinegar is obtained from a natural process of fermentation, with no preservatives or chemicals added. Studies link coconut sap vinegar to a plethora of health benefits, including improved heart health.

Coconut vinegar (sukang niyog), available in health food stores, is made from either coconut water or coconut floral sap, with coconut water vinegar considered as lower in quality.

Coconut water, called buko juice by Filipinos, is the clear liquid inside young green coconuts. Most of its composition is water and therefore, compared to coconut cream and coconut milk, it contains far fewer calories and hardly any saturated fat. While it is generally consumed as a drink in the Philippines, coconut water can also be used in food preparations to infuse dishes with a natural subtle sweetness. Coconut water is widely available in mainstream supermarkets, usually in cartons. Go for the purest young coconut water you can find that's not from concentrate.

Coconut, young shredded (kinayod na buko) is available frozen in 1 lb (500 g) packs at Filipino grocers. Unlike the mature coconuts, the meat from young coconuts is tender and silky.

Eggplant (talong) The Asian eggplant found in the Philippines is long and thin. It is less bitter and more tender than the globe variety. It also cooks faster, and so absorbs less oil. The fiber content in eggplants may help decrease levels of "bad" cholesterol as well as the associated risk of heart disease.

Fish sauce (patis) is widely available in regular supermarkets. It gives dishes a salty and umami punch, but use it sparingly as researchers have found that one tablespoon of fish sauce could pack up to 96 percent of our maximum recommended daily sodium intake, making it the saltiest offender among Asian sauces. (Salt content may vary depending on the brand, so check the nutritional information on the label.)

Glutinous or sticky rice flour (galapong malagkit) is flour made from glutinous rice, also known as sticky or sweet rice. Like rice flour, it is gluten free, but with a higher starch content. It has a sticky and chewy texture when cooked.

Green papaya is a papaya harvested before it is ripe. Its flesh is whitish and crisp, unlike the orange flesh of ripe papaya. In Philippine cooking, it's used as a vegetable rather than a fruit. Research shows that including more papaya in your diet may boost heart health.

Jackfruit (langka) is available either ripe or young. Ripe, sweet, yellow jackfruit is canned in syrup and used for an assortment of desserts. Young, unripe jackfruit is canned in brine and often used by vegans as a meat substitute. In Filipino cooking it is more commonly used as a vegetable. Fresh jackfruit is a good source of potassium and Vitamin C.

Mangoes (mangga) Green and yellow mangoes are the same fruit in different stages of maturity. Mangoes are packed with fiber, potassium and vitamins that can help toward keeping the arteries in great shape.

Milkfish (bangus) is available frozen. It is considered the national fish of the Philippines and a great source of omega-3 and fatty acids, believed to have benefits for the heart. Bangus is a bony fish, but you can buy it already deboned and butterflied. Well-frozen fish may have the same nutritional quality as fresh fish.

Moringa leaves (malunggay), also known as horseradish leaves, are the foliage of the drumstick (horseradish) tree. They are available fresh or frozen. Moringa is a nutrient powerhouse also lauded for its cholesterol-lowering effects.

Mung beans (monggo), also called balatong in some parts of the Philippines, are tiny pulses. They are used in both sweet and savory dishes in Philippine cooking. Major supermarkets stock dried mung beans in the aisle where you find lentils, beans and other legumes. You can also find them at health food stores and online. Mung beans have antioxidant and anti-inflammatory properties and may lower the risk of diabetes and heart disease.

Nipa palm vinegar (sukang nipa/sukang paombong) is fermented nipa palm sap.

Pandan (screwpine) leaves are the long sword-shaped leaves of the tropical pandan plant. They are not edible and are mainly used to impart aroma and flavor to food.

Rice flour (galapong bigas) is widely available in regular supermarkets. It is gluten free, so when mixed with cornstarch for batter instead of wheat or all-purpose flour, it absorbs less moisture and fat, making a lighter, crispier and less greasy crust.

Sugarcane (tubo) is available fresh or frozen. It is the raw ingredient of most processed sugar. Unprocessed, it hosts a variety of nutrients that are good for the heart.

Taro leaves (dahon ng gabi) are the heart-shaped leaves of the taro plant, available dried and shredded, or whole packed in plastic bags in Filipino or Asian grocers. They're known to be high in potassium, which helps regulate healthy heartbeats and manage high blood pressure.

Ube purple yam is a vividly violet tuber available in Filipino or Asian grocery stores, ready grated and frozen, or powdered in packs. It's a great source of antioxidants linked to protection against cancer, high blood pressure and inflammation.

Vinegar see **Cane vinegar**, **Coconut sap vinegar**, **Coconut vinegar** and **Nipa palm vinegar**

Water spinach or morning glory (kangkong) is also known as swamp cabbage. It grows both on land and in water. Leafy greens contain essential nutrients that protect against heart disease.

Healthy Seasoning Tips

Seasonings are often high in sodium, added sugar and unhealthy fats. For healthier alternatives, try using some of the seasoning ingredients listed here.

Coconut aminos is made from fermented coconut sap mixed with sea salt. Its salty, savory, umami-rich and subtly sweet taste is a match made in heaven for Filipino food. By using coconut aminos instead of soy sauce, we can reduce our sodium intake by up to 73 percent (depending on the brand). It can also sweeten dishes without needing to add more sugar. Some grocery stores stock coconut aminos near the spices and seasonings in the health food aisle, or next to the soy sauce. It can also be purchased from health food stores and online retailers.

Coconut sugar or coconut palm sugar is brown sugar made from the dehydrated sap of coconut palm. It is less processed than refined sugar and therefore contains more nutrients. It also has a lower glycemic index than most other sugars, making it a better alternative if you want to avoid blood sugar spikes. It is, however, still sugar and should be used sparingly.

Dates are an excellent sugar substitute because they are naturally sweet and high in fiber. Their antioxidant content may help prevent heart disease. Dried, pitted dates are widely available in regular supermarkets. Date syrup and date sugar are available in health food stores and from online shops. Although they are still considered as added sugar, they are less processed than refined sugar and therefore slightly more nutritious.

Dried Kombu or kelp is a type of dried seaweed that can infuse dishes with umami flavor and nutrients with a lot less sodium than store-bought broths. It can be found in East Asian markets and health food stores.

Nutritional yeast has a savory, cheesy and nutty flavor. This flavor booster, low in sodium and saturated fats has been acclaimed for lowering blood cholesterol. However, nutritionists advise to introduce nutritional yeast gradually into the diet to avoid possible side effects. Nutritional yeast is sold as flakes, granules or powder in canisters or jars, often found in the spice section of supermarkets or health food stores. Caution: not recommended for individuals with yeast sensitivity or allergy, inflammatory bowel disease (IBD), glaucoma, gout and hypertension.

Seasoning with Salt

The average dietary salt intake of most people is 9–12 grams of salt per day. The Filipino diet has an average of 12–15 grams salt per day. How much salt is just right? The American Heart Association recommends NO MORE THAN 5.75 grams, roughly 1 teaspoon of salt or 2,300 mg/day of sodium for adults. For those with high blood pressure, the recommended limit is much lower.

Salt is a culinary asset. Aside from imparting taste, it has the power to intensify the flavors of a dish. But it should be used wisely. The goal is to use less to flavor more. Here are some tips on when to salt, which have been applied to the recipes in this book:

- **When cooking,** add salt early, while the meat is still raw. The muscle fibers of meat clump and dry up as the meat cooks, preventing optimal absorption of taste and flavor.

- **When roasting,** toss vegetables with salt and oil just before cooking.

- **When sautéing,** salt vegetables at the end to prevent them from turning limp and soggy due to the moisture-drawing effect of salt. We want crunch and caramelization in our sautéed veggies.

- **Beans** Salt dried beans by adding salt to the soaking water. Aside from flavoring them, salt softens their cell walls. Make sure, however, to rinse thoroughly before cooking. For beans or pulses that don't require soaking, salt at the early stage of cooking.

- **Meat** Salt proteins in advance, allowing the salt to sink in. For meats such as a whole chicken, leave the salt-rubbed bird overnight in the fridge or at least a few hours before cooking. For more delicate proteins, such as fish, salting for about 5 minutes before cooking is enough. If left too long, it could result in a dry and tough fish. For a flavorful salt rub, try the Pinoy Powder recipe on this page.

- **Soups, salads, sauces and marinades** Salt dissolves faster in water than in fat. In soups, salt can be added later in the soup cooking process because it will dissolve more quickly. However, when preparing dressings for salad, sauces or marinades, dissolve salt first with acid or water before adding the oil.

- **Vegetables** Lightly salt the cooking or blanching water (just enough water to cook the veggies) before adding the vegetables. Not only does this season vegetables better, it fractionally cuts down cooking time and prevents vegetables from diffusing most of their nutrients out into the cooking liquid.

Pinoy Powder

Swap store-bought rubs, bouillon powder or cubes, broths and seasoning for this easy to make, low-sodium Pinoy Powder. This powder adds luya (ginger) and luyang dilaw (turmeric), common ingredients in Philippine cooking, into the mix. Both tubers have been found to host antioxidants that may help prevent heart disease and cancer, especially when paired with garlic, like in this recipe.

PREPARATION TIME 5 minutes
YIELD 2 cups

1 cup nutritional yeast
2 tablespoons garlic powder
2 tablespoons onion powder
2 tablespoons dried basil
2 tablespoons dried rosemary
2 tablespoons dried thyme
2 tablespoons sea salt
1½ tablespoons ginger powder
1½ tablespoons turmeric powder
1 tablespoon pepper

1 In a blender or food processor, combine all ingredients into a fine powder. Store in an airtight container. It will keep for up to 6 months.
2 To make broth, mix Pinoy Powder with hot water to make the quantity called for in the recipe you are using.

PER TABLESPOON OF PINOY POWDER (INCLUDING YEAST)
CALORIES 14.5KCAL | FATS 0.16G | SATURATED FAT 0.1G
PROTEIN 2.42G | CARBOHYDRATES 1.79G | FIBER 0.8G
SODIUM 441MG | SUGARS 0.16G

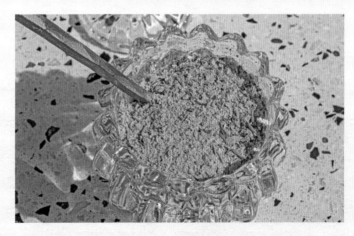

Flavor-Enhancing Techniques

Acid On its own, acid might not be particularly palatable, but when splashed on savory and sweetish dishes, it enhances the saltiness, umami and sweetness in lightly seasoned food. Notice how squeezes of calamansi or citrus juice at the end of cooking or right before serving dishes such as pancit, lugaw and sisig lift the dish to a whole new level, or how a sawsawan (dipping sauce) of vinegar adds zing to daing na bangus, longanisa or lumpia. Even a mung bean stew sings when drizzled with vinegar!

Adobo o pinalambot (braising or stewing) Stewing and braising require time and patience but little effort because you practically don't have to do anything while the food is left to simmer. Stews and braises build flavor by melting the collagen in meat without drying it out. To intensify flavor, add aromatics such as Guisa Ice Cubes (page 17) and flavorful low-sodium broth, such as Pinoy Powder (page 15).

Browning When the proteins and sugars in food are heated, the browning that takes place is called the Maillard reaction, producing new flavors and aromas. Browning via dry methods of cooking, such as grilling, barbecuing, pan-frying, sautéing and roasting conjures heights of heavenly flavor. This technique is also the first step to developing flavor when stewing or braising, such as cooking adobo. To brown the surface of proteins, sear it first on high heat. Make sure that the meat is dry,

the pan is hot and that you do not overcrowd the pan. The absence of moisture is integral to browning. Once browned, add the liquid then cook it through using gentle heat.

Caramelizing Caramelization takes place when heat reacts with the sugar in or on the food. As moisture evaporates, a rich and delicious layer of browning forms. Caramelize vegetables, fruits and marinated ingredients to add depth to their flavor.

Garlic and aromatics Garlic gives an exciting aroma and loads of flavor to almost everything we cook. When fried and used as a topping, it also adds texture. Garlic is a potent cooking ingredient with a myriad of proven heart health benefits, including lowering blood pressure and cholesterol. Cooking, however, destroys most of garlic's medicinal properties. To get the benefit of its nutrients, it is recommended to wait at least 10 minutes after crushing, chopping or mincing the bulb before cooking it. This gives time for a more heat-stable enzyme called allicin to form. Flavor can be further ramped up by using other aromatics, such as onion, celery, carrots (see Guisa Ice Cubes on page 17) and herbs and spices.

Guisa (stir-frying or sautéing) The benefits of stir-frying are twofold: nutrients are retained due to fast cooking, and flavor is enhanced by cooking with little oil, high heat and frequent stirring. Stir-frying accelerates rapid moisture removal to induce caramelization or Maillard reaction. A kawali (wok) is the ideal vessel for sautés because its curved sides allow easy stirring of ingredients around its surface.

Guisa or Filipino stir-fries always begin with sautéing aromatics. This recipe for Guisa Ice Cubes can serve as a foundation of many Filipino sautés and stews. Prepping a big batch of Guisa Ice Cubes (especially when the vegetables are at their freshest), freezing them in ice cube trays and plopping them into the pan as a flavor booster, makes cooking throughout the week or month a lot easier. Guisa Ice Cubes come in handy when making dishes like torta (omelet), pancit (stir-fried rice noodles), stewed monggo (mung beans) and many more.

Marinating Marinades consist of salt, acid, oil, sugar and flavorings. They season meat mainly on the outside and slightly on the inside. Only the salt component, and perhaps the sugar to a lesser extent, penetrate within, but rarely over an eighth of an inch deep even after 24 hours of soaking. Therefore, to amplify flavor, cut meat into smaller pieces to increase the surface area exposed to the marinade. This is why the Filipino pork barbecue on sticks is so tasty. Besides surface treatment, marinating can enhance the flavor of meat and vegetables, such as eggplant and mushrooms during cooking through browning and caramelization.

Pinais (cooking in banana leaves)
Steaming, roasting or grilling food wrapped in banana leaves gives food a glorious aroma and taste.

Guisa Ice Cubes

PREPARATION TIME 45 minutes
YIELD approximately 35 frozen cubes

¼ cup olive oil
1 medium head garlic, minced
2 large yellow onions, finely chopped
4 medium carrots, finely chopped
6 celery stalks, finely chopped
2 large tomatoes, finely chopped
1 teaspoon sea salt
1 teaspoon garlic powder
1 teaspoon onion powder
1 teaspoon freshly ground pepper

1 Heat the oil in a large sauté pan on medium-high heat until it shimmers.
2 Add the garlic and onions. Stir-fry for about 12 minutes or until the onions start to caramelize.
3 Add the carrots, stirring often for about 8 minutes, until the carrots start to caramelize.
4 Add the rest of the ingredients. Cook for 5 minutes or until the tomatoes melt into the mixture. Remove from the heat and allow to cool.
5 Spoon the mixture into ice cube trays with lids. Once frozen, you can transfer to zip-top bags and return to the freezer. They will keep for at least 2 months. Defrost before use or drop frozen into the pan on low heat to defrost.

PER CUBE **CALORIES** 28KCAL | **FATS** 2.13G | **PROTEIN** 0.32G
CHOLESTEROL 0MG | **CARBOHYDRATES** 2.05G | **FIBER** 0.5G
SODIUM 75MG | **SUGARS** 0.88G | **SATURATED FAT** 0.3G

CHAPTER 1

Kanin at Agahan
Rice and Morning Meals

Learn how to cook good rice, and you're halfway to making a sumptuous Filipino meal — eating with rice, to most Filipinos, defines a meal. The traditional Filipino breakfast, rather than just "breaking a fast," is hearty enough to invigorate the body even for the toughest of grinds. Sometimes it's in the form of a silog ("si" comes from the first syllable of *sinangag* garlic rice, and "log" from the last syllable of itlog egg), teamed up with a pre-prepped ulam (a dish served with rice), such as daing na bangus marinated milkfish, longanisa Filipino sausage, tocino cured ham, tapa marinated beef, dried fish or yesterday's adobo. Filipino breakfast food, like silog and lugaw rice porridge, are not exclusively eaten in the morning, but any time of the day.

Recipes in this chapter are closely in line with the 2019 American Heart Health program, which recommends that a main dish should contain no more than 600 mg of sodium, 500 calories and 2 teaspoons of added sugars per serving.

Sinaing
Stovetop Steamed Rice

Sinaing, meaning cooked rice, comes from the root word "saing," which refers to the way Filipinos boil and steam this staple grain. In the beginning, our ancestors cooked rice in bamboo tubes placed directly on the fire or buried under it, or in leaf-lined earthen pots set over burning wood. Rice had its designated cooking vessel and this vessel was not used to cook anything else.

In the 1900s, when the Philippines was under American rule, a variety of rice-cooking methods were introduced through cookbooks pushed forward in Philippine public schools. Nevertheless, sinaing (rice cooked the "saing" way) prevails in Filipino kitchens. Over the years, technology has made strides in revolutionizing rice cooking—these days you're unlikely to come across a cooking pot like the one pictured on this page! Yet, unlike many of the Filipino ulam (dishes served with rice), sinaing's ingredients (rice and water), cooking method (boiling and steaming) and soul (unadulterated simplicity) remain unchanged.

Filipinos cook rice using just the right amount of water to boil and steam the grain until all the liquid has been absorbed. The rice is cooked to perfection when it's tender and fluffy and each grain holds its shape. Sometimes, scrunched up pieces of fragrant pandan (screwpine) leaves, known as the "vanilla of the East," are added to the pot to impart flavor. Almost always, no salting (meaning more sodium allowance for the ulam!), seasoning, oiling, mixing or draining excess water is involved. Simple and easy. The big question is, how much water is "just right"? It depends on the amount of rice cooked, the cooking vessel and the method of cooking. Rice cookers and Instant Pots are a godsend as they keep the latter two variables constant. Hence, the outcome is the same almost all the time.

But what if we have neither? We need to learn how to cook rice on a stovetop.

I learned that following a fixed water-to-rice ratio even for cooking the same type of rice doesn't work all the time. Why? Because it's not the absorption rate that is erratic — it's the evaporation rate. How much water escapes depends on how big the cooking vessel is, how tightly the lid fits and the source of heat. This means that even if I cook 4 cups of rice in the same pot I used to cook 2 cups of rice in exactly the same way, I don't need to add twice the amount of water. The guide on the facing page will help you work out the right amount of water to cook plain rice the way you like it every time.

1. **Measure the amount of rice you want to cook and place it in a pot with a tight lid**. Make sure the pot is big enough for the quantity of rice you normally cook.

You can use white rice or whole grain rice (brown, black, red, etc.) If using whole grain, soak it overnight in warm water with one teaspoon of acid such as vinegar or lemon juice for every cup of rice. This is recommended to help break down the hard-to-digest components of the grain and reduce phytic acid, a substance that impairs mineral absorption.

2. **Rinse the rice thoroughly with warm water and drain well.** Rinsing may help get rid of any traces of arsenic present on the grains. It also alters the texture of the cooked rice by washing off layers of surface starch to prevent the grains from sticking together. If well-separated grains are what you're after, rinse more. If you're using enriched rice and don't want to wash off the vitamins and nutrients, rinse less.

3. **Establish the ideal water-to-rice ratio that works for you.** Cook 1 cup (200 g) of rice at the ratio of 1.75:1 (1¾ cups [420 ml] of water to 1 cup of rice). This ratio works for me. Add the water to the rice and place over medium-high heat uncovered. Once it starts to boil, cover and reduce the heat to medium low. Leave until the grains have completely absorbed the water and become opaque and tender, about 15–20 minutes for white rice, and longer for

colored rice. If no more water is left and the rice looks uncooked, add measured amounts of water in small increments (e.g., ¼ cup [60 ml]). Take note of how much is added. Let cook until the water has evaporated and the rice is cooked. Leave to sit for 10 minutes.

4. **Find out the evaporation rate.** Work out the evaporation rate by subtracting the number of cups of uncooked rice used from the number of cups of water used. The difference is the evaporation rate. For example, if your ideal water-to-rice ratio is 1.75: 1 then your calculation will be as follows:

Amount of evaporation =
1.75 cups water – 1 cup rice = 0.75 cup

5. **Figure out the amount of water needed to cook different quantities of rice.** Always use the same pot, lid and method regardless of the amount of rice you are cooking. The two values to consider are:

1) Absorption rate = 1:1 (this is more or less the same for any type of rice)
2) Amount of evaporation

For example, If you want to cook 2 cups (400 g) rice:

Amount of water = absorption rate (1:1) +
                   evaporation rate (e.g., 0.75 cup)
                 = 2 cups water + 0.75 cup water
                 = 2.75 cups water

Full Bellies, Full Hearts

Dorina Lazo Gilmore-Young

Dorina Lazo Gilmore-Young is the author of *Cora Cooks Pancit* **and** *Chasing God's Glory*. **She's also a speaker, podcaster at Eat Pray Run and spoken word artist. Dorina and her husband Shawn are raising three multiracial daughters who love to travel and cook together. Here she shares how she prepares her good ol' sinaing using her favorite rice variety and "the new rice cooker."**

> *"Grandma's morning rhythm always started with making a pot of coffee and starting a batch of rice in her well-loved rice cooker."*

Whenever I get a whiff of rice steaming in a rice cooker, I'm transported back to my childhood. My grandma's morning rhythm always started with making a pot of coffee and starting a batch of rice in her well-loved rice cooker with that signature peeling enamel along the bottom.

She'd rinse the rice a few times. Then she'd measure the water using the first knuckle method that most Asians swear by before letting me press start on the rice cooker. The rice would turn out perfectly every time.

For snacks, Grandma would make my brother and me sticky rice balls. She would send all her grandkids off on trips with a little container of rice balls. It was something simple, but through the years I realized that little gesture was Grandma's way of sending us out with love. She wanted to ensure our bellies and hearts were full.

Rice is a staple in many cultures across the world. Some cultures mix rice with beans or serve it with protein, sauces and veggies spooned on top. For Filipinos, rice is a symbol of warmth, comfort, safety and home. And the kitchen was the place where stories unfolded. The kitchen always held a centrifugal force, drawing different generations of our family together. I loved to listen to the stories told by Grandma, Mama and aunties of growing up in Hawaii and later raising their kids together in the Bay Area. Grandma's family emigrated from the Philippines to the Hawaiian Islands when she was a girl. Their Filipino culture blended in with the locals' for

> *"As a young mother, I longed to recreate that special bond with my own daughters. [...] I began to do the work of recording the family recipes. These would be the flavors and ingredients that would tell the stories of our heritage."*

they embodied the Hawaiian spirit of aloha that extended welcoming arms to all and made strangers into ohana (family).

Grandma would tilt her head back and giggle like a schoolgirl as she unfurled her stories of growing up an island girl and how she met my grandpa in Kona. She sparked my curiosity with her tidbits about traveling the world and trying the cuisines of other countries.

Grandma taught us to cherish our Asian Pacific heritage. Our people and our cuisine are a mix of cultures. Grandma was proud of her ethnic mosaic of Filipino, Polynesian, Spanish, Portuguese, Chinese and other cultures. Despite some of the difficult history the Philippines has endured, Grandma saw the blending of groups of people as a gift.

It wasn't until later in life, when Grandma and several of my aunties soared to heaven that I realized how treasured that time together in the kitchen was for me. As a young mother, I longed to recreate that special bond with my own daughters. I realized most of my friends did not have the experience I did.

I began to do the work of recording the family recipes. These would be the flavors and ingredients that would tell the stories of our heritage.

Now I invite my daughters, my mama, my sister, my nieces and nephews and many friends into my kitchen. We serve up rice, pancit, lumpia, adobo chicken and other Filipino favorites.

I continue to serve this handful of dishes at my table because it's important to me. Every day we have the opportunity to continue the legacy passed down to us by our parents and grandparents when we gather in the kitchen to make these recipes, savor these foods and tell these stories. We keep their values of family, hospitality, generosity and diversity alive.

Up until the end of her life, Grandma was still making her pot of coffee and rice in the morning. I like to imagine her in Heaven today serving up coffee and rice balls to angels and friends.

Kanin Instant Pot Rice

According to Dorina, her grandparents always kept their rice cooker out on the counter because it was used so often. As she was growing up, her parents also used a rice cooker to cook rice. Now that she has kids of her own, her appliance of choice is the Instant Pot. She loves the way it cooks rice! She likes to use jasmine rice, but she was raised on Mahatma long-grain rice from the big bags with the red writing.

PREPARATION TIME 15 minutes
YIELD about 3 cups (600 g) rice

1 Pour 1 cup (200 g) of uncooked rice into a bowl. Cover with water to rinse it. Swirl around with your fingers then slowly pour out the water into the sink. Repeat. Pour the washed rice into the Instant Pot and add 1½ cups of water.
2 Lock and seal the Instant Pot and press the RICE function. It will cook the rice for 10 minutes. (You can also press the MANUAL button and choose 10 minutes as your quantity for cooking time.)
3 After the Instant Pot beeps, allow the rice to sit in the pot for an extra five minutes before unsealing and serving.

> **STORAGE TIP**
> Keep cooled cooked rice in the refrigerator for 4–7 days in an airtight container, or freeze in zip-top bags for up to 6 months. Reheat thoroughly in the microwave for 3–5 minutes until piping hot throughout.

"Whenever I get a whiff of rice steaming in a rice cooker, I'm transported back to my childhood."

PER CUP OF COOKED RICE
CALORIES 225KCAL
FATS 0.41G | SATURATED FAT 0.1G
PROTEIN 4.4G | CARBOHYDRATES 49.3G
FIBER 0.8G | SODIUM 1MG
SUGARS 0.07G

When Life Gives You Vinegar

Cheryl Baun

Chef Paolo Mendoza, a 2023 James Beard Award semi-finalist, and his wife, Cheryl Baun, are the couple behind the restaurant Karenderya in Nyack, New York. Paolo worked in high profile restaurants in New York City and the Hudson Valley before Karenderya, while Cheryl, the restaurant's manager, has translated her skills from her career in nonprofit management into hospitality.

> *"I take a moment to go over and say hello to the guests [...] Creating a place that feels homey and welcoming is a central guiding principle of our business."*

I look up to give my eyes a break from reading the small print on a stack of bills. I scan the room. Nothing much has changed since the restaurant opened over one year ago: a carved wooden deity called bulul, believed by the Ifugao — a minority ethnic group in the Philippines — to guard rice fields and granaries, sits on the bar counter. Mismatched chairs and benches complementing bare wooden tables lend the place a carinderia (roadside Filipino eatery) vibe, reminiscent of the ones Paolo, my husband and the restaurant's chef, remembers from his childhood in Pasay City. Scribbled on the chalkboard wall is a Cesar Chavez quote, "If you really want to make a friend, go to someone's house and eat with him ... the people who give you their food give you their heart."

Everything in the room is pretty much the same ... except today, like yesterday and the past few days, I can count the diners with the fingers of one hand. In fact, out of the two tables occupied, one is taken by me, the restaurant owner, and my two kids. We have entered the slow season. Paolo and I have already dipped several times into our reserve funds and worn down the generosity of our families to keep the restaurant running. If business continues like this, I have no idea how the restaurant can stay afloat.

We had always daydreamed about opening a restaurant. But it was just that, a dream; not something that we expected to turn into reality — until the summer of 2016. Paolo quit

> "We never set out to be the best in America. We just strive to be the best according to our own standards and to do it honestly and with integrity."

his job at a prominent restaurant and decided to start up Karenderya, a casual Filipino-inspired restaurant. Paolo was brave, but he was no daredevil; he jumped out of a plane, because he knew he had a parachute — my well-paying job at a national healthcare nonprofit.

Four months later, the parachute ripped. I lost my job. It became clear that Karenderya was our hope and our future. Well, they say when life gives you lemons, you make lemonade. In our case, you can say that life gave us vinegar, so we made daing.

I take a moment to go over and say hello to the guests at the other table, something I customarily do. Creating a place that feels homey and welcoming is a central guiding principle of our business.

Back in July 2017, when we opened, we enjoyed a good amount of local press attention, an outpouring of support from the community, and customers in droves. Even then, we made it a point to get to know our customers by name and quickly gained regulars and cheerleaders. But as winter set in, the number of customers started to dwindle.

The door swings open. In walks a man with a tousled mane and a beautiful woman pushing a stroller with twin babies. They settle down at a table, before the man comes up to the counter

to order a sampling of items from our menu. He's obviously not Filipino, but is knowledgeable about the cuisine. Paolo pops out of the kitchen and the three of us chat for a while about Filipino food. We've never met this man before but we recognize him from Instagram. He's Jeff Gordinier, the food and drinks editor of *Esquire* magazine!

A few weeks later, we get a congratulatory email from Jeff. He has included Karenderya on his annual Best New Restaurants in America list! In his 2018 Esquire article, he describes our pork belly as "braised to crispy meltiness atop garlic rice," our shrimp adobo as "shrimp aswim in coconut broth that tastes like French cream," and our cassava-jackfruit cake, "like a cobbler in which the topping and the filling have magically merged."

This was never part of the plan. We never dreamed of receiving these kinds of accolades. We never set out to be the best in America. We just strive to be the best according to our own standards and to do it honestly and with integrity. Normally uncomfortable in the spotlight, Paolo cautiously allows himself to enjoy this moment. But I focus on this sentence in Jeff's email to us: "Thank you for making me and my family feel so at home ..." I now know that we earned our spot on the list.

Daing na Bangus
Pan-Fried Marinated Milkfish

The word "daing" refers to a method of preserving fish usually by salting and drying. Daing na bangus, however, is not dried but marinated. Marinate the bangus (milkfish), cook the rice, mince the garlic, prepare the salad dressing the night before and you're off to a good start in the morning.

PREPARATION TIME 15 minutes + 8 hours marinating time
YIELD 4 servings

DAING NA BANGUS
8 cloves garlic, crushed
½ cup (120 g) white vinegar
½ teaspoon black peppercorns, crushed
⅓ teaspoon sea salt
4 frozen deboned and butterflied baby milkfish, thawed, about 1 lb (500 g) total
2 tablespoons vegetable oil

TOMATO-CUCUMBER SALAD
1 teaspoon minced red onion
1½ tablespoons calamansi or lime juice
1½ teaspoons patis (fish sauce)
1 teaspoon minced jalapeno, optional
Freshly ground pepper to taste
½ cup (75 g) grape tomatoes
½ cup (65 g) cucumber, diced

Nutritional information for this dish, along with its rice and egg accompaniments, is given on the next page.

1 Mix the garlic, vinegar, pepper and salt in a bowl to make the marinade. Place the milkfish in a ziplock bag. Pour the marinade into the bag and ensure all the fish is in contact with the marinade. Let the air out of the bag and seal.
2 Refrigerate and leave to marinate for at least 8 hours or overnight.
3 Prepare the Tomato-Cucumber Salad. Mix the onion, juice, patis, jalapeno (if using) and pepper together in a bowl. Add the tomatoes and stir. Let it sit for at least 15 minutes. Toss the cucumber with this mixture just a few minutes before serving to retain its crunch.
4 Heat the oil over medium-high heat until it shimmers. Shake off excess liquid from the marinated fish.
5 Pan-fry the fish skin side first until crisp and golden, about 1–2 minutes. Flip the fish over and cook until golden brown, about 1–2 minutes. Drain in paper towels. Keep warm until ready to serve.

Silog: Sinangag at Itlog
Cauliflower Fried Rice with Sunny Side-Up Egg
by Jacqueline Chio-Lauri

Sinangag from "sangag" means to toast grain. Here, cauliflower, naturally high in fiber and nutrients, is added to the mix. The beauty of blending it with rice is that it goes undetected.

PREPARATION TIME 15 minutes
YIELD 4 servings

1½ cups (300 g) cooked rice, preferably refrigerated leftover rice
1 tablespoon olive oil
4 cloves garlic, minced
1 cup (120 g) riced cauliflower, or 4 oz (120 g) cauliflower florets blitzed in a blender
4 small eggs
1 teaspoon water
Pinch of garlic powder
Pinch of freshly ground pepper
Pinch of salt

1 Make the sinangag: Crumble the rice with your hands to break up the lumps. Heat the oil over medium-high heat in a nonstick skillet with a lid until it shimmers. Add the garlic and stir-fry until lightly golden. Remove about a quarter of the garlic using a slotted spoon. Set aside.

2 Add rice the and the riced cauliflower to the skillet and stir-fry. Continue stirring for about 5 minutes until the rice is slightly golden and the garlic is mixed evenly. Transfer to serving dishes or containers.

3 Make the eggs: Lower the heat to medium. Crack the eggs into the same skillet making sure they are evenly spaced. Sprinkle with the teaspoon of water. Immediately cover with a lid.

4 When the egg whites are completely opaque, about 1–2 minutes, place a fried egg on top of each portion of rice. Season with garlic powder, pepper and salt and sprinkle with the remaining toasted garlic.

5 Serve with Daing na Bangus and Tomato-Cucumber Salad (see previous page).

PER SERVING OF DAING NA BANGUS (PREVIOUS PAGE) AND SILOG (THIS PAGE) **CALORIES** 417KCAL | **FATS** 23.98G
SATURATED FAT 4.5G
PROTEIN 27.7G | **CARBOHYDRATES** 22.17G
FIBER 3G | **SODIUM** 564MG | **SUGARS** 6.94G

MAKE-AHEAD TIP
Portion cooked daing (page 27) and sinangag in microwavable or heatproof containers. Cool then refrigerate. Will keep for up to 5 days. Reheat in the microwave for 1–2 minutes. Simply add an egg and Tomato-Cucumber Salad (page 27) and your breakfast is ready in a jiff. Alternatively, freeze cooked daing and sinangag in freezer-safe containers for up to 1 month.

My Kitchen Karma

Kathy Vega Hardy

Accountant turned cook Kathy Vega Hardy started her food truck, A Taste of the Philippines, in Denver in 2012 and competed on Food Network's hit shows *Cutthroat Kitchen* (twice) and *Chopped*. In 2018, she moved to Chicago and in 2020 opened her A Taste of the Philippines restaurant inside the Chicago French Market.

> *"She said that this was my karma for all of those times I didn't help out in the kitchen — a karma of the most delicious kind."*

130. That was the number when I looked down at the scale. I am just five feet tall, and the fact that my weight was now 130 pounds meant my health had stopped being a priority for me.

It was 2007. I was an accountant in Springfield, Illinois and most of my days were spent at a desk tackling spreadsheets, balancing financial statements and writing reports. My coworkers and I often sipped cups of coffee spiked with Baileys. Nights were often spent at bars, downing too much booze and nurturing that I don't give a f*ck attitude many of us sport in our early twenties.

I never ran out of drinking buddies, but close friends were in short supply. I was dealing with family issues and couldn't find the support I needed. And to top it all off, I was wrapped up in an on-and-off toxic relationship of almost seven years. I needed to get away.

So, I took off. I traveled eight hundred miles to visit a couple of my girlfriends in the picturesque town of Boulder, Colorado with views of the majestic Rocky Mountains rearing into the sky. The air was sweeter and the pace of life slower. By the second day, a new sense of clarity took over. All the white noise of family drama and boyfriend issues had been quieted, and my body responded favorably to being outside and being active, something that wasn't always easy in small-town southern Illinois.

When I returned to Springfield, I handed in my notice at work. I packed a twenty-two-foot long yellow moving van with everything I owned. I drove back to Boulder leaving family, friends and

> ## "Boulder's health-nut atmosphere inspired me to try ingredients I wouldn't normally have used [...] My healthy lifestyle stuck, my love of cooking continued to grow."

life as I'd known it behind. I was twenty-four years old.

I knew no one in Boulder except for the girls I had visited. I got a new accounting job, but I had a lot of time on my hands when I wasn't working. I started running when I was bored, which was often. Every day, I would run a little bit farther, a little bit faster. I also began eating healthier, bringing lots of lean meats and vegetables into my diet.

Before long, I was hooked on my new healthy lifestyle. There was one problem however. The Filipino food I felt at home with didn't seem to fit into my new healthy regimen.

Cooking hadn't always been my favorite thing. My mother, a chef, used to set me and my siblings up in lumpia spring-roll assembly lines in our kitchen when we were young. If you ask anyone in my family, they'll tell you I was always the one who was "sick" during lumpia rolling time, the one to sneak out and meet up with friends. But with all this free time on my hands, the strong hankering for the food I grew up eating led me to experiment with creating new versions of Filipino dishes. Boulder's health-nut atmosphere inspired me to try ingredients I wouldn't normally have used, substituting them for less healthy ones in my favorite Filipino meals.

110. That's about the number of longanisa sausages I made before I got the recipe right. My healthy lifestyle stuck, my love of cooking continued to grow and the number on the scale doesn't matter much. Five years later after moving to Boulder, I walked away from a nearly

decade-long career in accounting and started my food business, serving my creations all over Denver. It became more popular than I had ever imagined. But that's another story. As I scooped one tablespoon after another of ground meat to shape into a longanisa sausage, my mother's words came to mind. She said that this was my karma for all of those times I didn't help out in the kitchen — a karma of the most delicious kind.

Skinless Longanisa
Turkey and Pork Breakfast Sausage

Longanisa, the traditional Filipino breakfast sausage, is typically made of ground pork, chunks of fat, salt, red food dye and brown sugar. This version takes on a cleaner spin by using a mix of ground turkey and ground pork, beetroot powder instead of food coloring, and dates instead of sugar for sweetness. Kathy's recipe yields very garlicky and mildly sweet sausages. Feel free to adjust the amount of garlic and dates to suit your taste.

PREPARATION TIME 30 minutes +
  8 hours marinating time
YIELD 6 servings

10 dates, pitted
1 tablespoon water
5–10 garlic cloves, minced
8 oz (250 g) ground turkey thigh
  (or ground chicken)
8 oz (250 g) ground pork, preferably 80:20
  lean to fat ratio
Pinch of fine sea salt
Pinch or more of freshly ground black
  pepper, to taste
1 tablespoon tamari, or coconut aminos
2 teaspoons organic beetroot powder, for
  color, optional
2 tablespoons extra virgin olive oil, divided

1 Place the dates in a handheld blender with the 1 tablespoon of water. Puree until smooth. Mix with the remaining ingredients, except half of the olive oil, in a large stainless-steel bowl, using a spatula or your hands.

2 Cover and leave to marinate in the fridge for at least 2 hours. 24 hours is best.

3 Scoop a tablespoonful of the meat mixture and roll into a 2-inch sausage log. Use gloves if needed to minimize contact with raw meat and avoid staining your hands red. Repeat until all the meat is formed into about 12 sausages. You can fry the longanisa right away or freeze them for later use rolled in greaseproof paper and placed in zip-top bags. Thaw before pan-frying.

4 To pan-fry, heat a 10-inch nonstick pan over medium-high heat. Add the remaining olive oil to coat the base. Lower the temperature to medium. Cook the sausages about half an inch (1 cm) apart in the pan. Make sure the meat is cooked all the way through or until a probe thermometer reads 165°F or 74°C.

5 Drain in kitchen paper towels when done. Serve with rice, half a boiled egg (page 34), lots of veggies and a sawsawan dipping sauce of vinegar seasoned with salt, pepper, and crushed garlic.

MAKE-AHEAD TIP
Portion cooked longanisa and rice in microwavable or heatproof containers. Cool then refrigerate. Will keep for up to 5 days. Reheat in the microwave for 1–2 minutes. Simply add half a boiled egg per portion and your choice of veggies and your breakfast is ready in a flash. Alternatively, freeze cooked longanisa an rice in freezer-safe containers for up to 1 month.

PER SERVING CALORIES 237KCAL | FATS 15.48G
SATURATED FAT 4.6G | PROTEIN 14.69G
CARBOHYDRATES 10.5G
FIBER 1.1G | SODIUM 277MG | SUGARS 7.65G

Healing with Lugaw

Zosima Margaret Fulwell

Half Filipino and half English, Zosima Margaret Fulwell aka Cooking with Mama Z has been serving Filipino Food to the north west of England since 2017. Zosima is a founding member of the Filipino Food Movement UK. In 2022, she co-opened a Malaysian-Filipino café in Manchester called Yes Lah.

> *"Lugaw has awakened my senses: sight, hearing, smell, taste, touch — and a sixth one I'd like to call awareness."*

I live in Manchester, one of the United Kingdom's largest cities. Unlike the Kingdom of Saudi Arabia, where I was born and raised under the care of a very religious Filipina mum and an English dad, here, I am free to do practically anything, free to practice any or no religion and free to be. I, however, am not always free from my thoughts or from my past.

A few years ago, at my flat in Manchester, I woke up in the middle of the night gripped by a tight feeling in my chest. It wasn't the first time this had happened. In fact, almost every night for nearly three months I'd been waking up with hatred raging in my heart — hatred toward my mum, then hatred toward myself for hating my mum. The hatred, fed by my thoughts and baggage from the past, which manifested itself in my dreams, took a life form of its own. It spiraled out of control fueling all sorts of awful emotions: anger, anxiety and depression. It made life unlivable.

It's hard to say exactly how or when my relationship with my mum broke down so completely. When I was a child, we were close. She was the most fashionable person I knew. She wore a jaw-grazing cropped bob — a stylish hairstyle in the nineties — and adorned herself with the finest jewelry. We had traveled often to Bataan, in the Philippines, where Mum comes from, and I'd learned to speak Tagalog during those visits.

Lugaw — a savory porridge — first earned its status as my healing food when I was about six

> **"The steam from the thick porridge opened up my nasal passages and awakened my senses [...] as pleasurable to the palate and throat as it was to the nose. It was as soothing as Mum's love."**

or seven years old. I woke up feeling dreadful one morning. Mum, after touching my forehead with the underside of her soft, perfectly manicured hand, let me skip school that day. As I snuggled up on the couch, clicking between MTV and Cartoon Network, eyes glued to the telly, the sounds and smells clued me to what mum was doing: the tap-tapping of the knife on the chopping board, the hissing of ingredients as they hit the hot oil and the ensuing aroma – that delicious smell released as garlic, onion and ginger were sautéed – it made my mouth water even though I was ill.

Mum set down a bowl of lugaw in front of me. The steam from the thick porridge opened up my nasal passages and awakened my senses. The taste of it was as pleasurable to the palate and throat as it was to the nose. It was as soothing as Mum's love. The whisper of the zesty, pungent flavor of ginger lingered and the bite from spring onion, garlic and calamansi zinged. I felt better – inside and outside!

Sadly, my relationship with Mum fizzled out over the years. Things became rocky in my adolescence and irreconcilable in my adulthood. I tried hard to suppress the emotions that sprang up from our broken relationship, but they resurfaced unconsciously in the form of nightmares, streaming into unwanted thoughts and emotions when I woke up in the morning. It was a vicious cycle.

But Mum had gifted me with the perfect feel-good food that I'd carry with me through life. As I did during childhood when feeling unwell, I still always turn to the soulful bowl of lugaw for comfort. Later on, I took a step further and decided to devote myself full-time to reconnecting with my Filipino heritage and cooking Filipino food. In the process of going deeper into my explorations of the cuisine and culture of my mum, I learned to put myself in Mum's shoes – from the way she was brought up to rules and beliefs imposed on her by the societies where she has lived. Eventually, some of my resentment toward her has melted into compassion.

Lugaw has awakened my senses: sight, hearing, smell, taste, touch – and a sixth one I'd like to call awareness. All together they lead the way to inner peace, a state of well-being I hope to pass on to people through food, including the woman who passed on to me the gift of lugaw – Mum.

Lugaw Oat Porridge with Soft-Boiled Egg

Lugaw, the Philippine's savory porridge, is said to have stemmed from congee introduced to the country by Chinese migrants. Zosima's breakfast version of lugaw, using oats, is quicker and easier to cook than the usual version made with rice. It's a low calorie, high-fiber alternative with just as much flavor and taste as the original. Fresh ingredients, such as ginger, garlic and lemon help fight off infections. You can pretty much add anything you want to it, making it suitable for both young and old. This way, lugaw transcends into a healing dish for everyone.

PREPARATION TIME 15 minutes
YIELD 2 servings

1 tablespoon olive oil
2 cloves garlic, minced
1 small white onion, minced
1-inch (2.5 cm) piece fresh ginger,
  peeled and chopped into strips
⅔ cup (60 g) porridge oats
1 teaspoon fish sauce
2 cups (480 ml) low sodium
  vegetable stock (or 1 tablespoon
  Pinoy Powder, page 15, mixed with
  2 cups water)
2 eggs
2 calamansi, halved or ½ lemon, cut
  into wedges
Salt, to taste
Freshly ground pepper, to taste

GARNISHES
Chopped fresh coriander
Chopped chili
Chopped spring onions
1 teaspoon sesame oil, optional
Handful steamed spinach or other
  greens, optional

PER SERVING CALORIES 295KCAL
FATS 15.59G | SATURATED FAT 2.3G
PROTEIN 11.83G
CARBOHYDRATES 28.78G | FIBER 4.2G
SODIUM 545MG | SUGARS 3.35G

1 Heat the oil in a saucepan over medium-high heat until it shimmers. Add the garlic and onion. Stir until the garlic turns golden and the onions translucent.
2 Add the ginger and stir for about a minute.
3 Add the oats and the fish sauce and stir until well mixed. Pour in the stock. Stir then leave to simmer, covered, over medium heat until the oats reach your desired texture and consistency, about 3 minutes or the recommended cooking time on the packet.
4 While the porridge simmers, prepare the soft-boiled eggs following the method in the box below.
5 Add a little water to the porridge if it is too thick. Squeeze in the calamansi or lemon juice and season with salt and pepper. Divide between two bowls.
6 Shell and split the eggs lengthwise and place on top of each bowl of lugaw. The yolk should be soft and oozy, making the lugaw creamier. Sprinkle with coriander, spring onion, chili and sesame oil, and add a little steamed spinach or other greens.

> HOW TO MAKE PERFECT SOFT-BOILED EGGS
> This method will give perfect eggs with a fully set white and a thick, runny yolk. Place about 2 cups (480 ml) of water (enough to submerge the eggs completely) in a small saucepan and bring to a roaring boil over high heat. Use a spoon to lower the eggs carefully one at a time into the boiling water. Reduce the heat to medium. Leave to simmer for 5 minutes. Run the eggs under cold water and set aside.

NUTRITION TIP
Pump up the nutrients by adding steamed greens like spinach as topping.

CHAPTER 2

Baon
Packed Lunches

Before clocks and watches, our forebears planned meal times according to the sun. For rice farmers, this meant hitting the fields early to get the work done before the heat became unbearable. Lunch, by and large, was prepared by the elder womenfolk, and was packed and delivered to the fields as "bahao," possibly the ancestor of "baon." Now, baon refers to any provision, including money, supplies and food brought to sustain oneself while away from home. The food we pack in our baon boxes are windows into our culture and the food we eat at home. Taking a baon lunch to school can be a catalyst of cultural awakening for a younger generation of Filipinos who have had little contact with the native land their parents and grandparents emigrated from. In this chapter, we explore a variety of nutritious and scrumptious lunch baon ideas that can be made ahead and are easy to prepare and pack on regular busy mornings.

Recipes in this chapter are closely in line with the 2019 American Heart Health program, which recommends that a main dish should contain no more than 600 mg of sodium, 500 calories, and 2 teaspoons of added sugars per serving.

Torta à la Lola

Jacqueline Chio-Lauri

Jacqueline Chio-Lauri is editor and lead author of the highly acclaimed
book *The New Filipino Kitchen* (2018) and the author of picture books
Mami King (2024) inspired by the story behind mami noodle soup,
and *The Hunger Fighter*, the story behind banana ketchup.
She lives in Manchester in the UK, her seventh country of residence.

> *"A fervent believer in the
> power of prayer, I spent
> more time praying than
> partaking of the gifts
> from His bounty."*

Growing up, I was used to getting jolted
out of bed by noises from the kitchen. Once, it
was the wailing of a child pleading for mercy and
pounding on stone. The cries were not from one of
my sisters, the children who lived with me under
the same roof as our lola — our grandma and
guardian. No, not this time. They were from a voice
actor in a radio soap opera. While the transistor
blasted, Lola pestled in a mortar the heads she had
severed from fresh raw shrimp. The rich, orangey
tomalley flavor she extracted perked up the taste
of many of her dishes.

"Lola, what's for lunch?" I asked in Kapampangan,
the language we spoke at home.

"Torta and alpang habichuelas."

Torta, a stovetop Filipino frittata was one of my
favorites. Alpang habichuelas, or sautéed green
beans, did nothing for me.

"Can I help you, Lola?"

"Not now. I'm busy. I'll give you something
to do later."

Even in her seventies, Lola maintained a slender
physique and an elegant posture as she toiled
away in our galley kitchen from daybreak till
siesta. Ailing cabinets sagging like slack jaws
hung above and under the fractured white-
tiled countertop. Rays of light rushed in like
paramedics through a small window from where
I peered out daily for a glimpse of the cross atop
Angeles City's cathedral.

While awaiting Lola's orders, I sprawled on the sofa
and flagellated the sole of my foot with a wooden

> **"The smell of aromatics sautéing in a glug of Baguio Oil danced in the air. In addition to minced beef, pork and shrimp, Lola packed her torta with an assortment of veggies. She emphasized the benefits of eating right."**

ruler — a form of sacrifice I performed to gain God's blessings. I stopped when I heard Lola approaching. Though inflicting physical pain on us children as punishment was common practice, children inflicting physical pain on themselves wasn't.

"Here, peel these," she said, putting some onions, cloves of garlic and a dull paring knife on the dining table. I was almost twelve, yet Lola still didn't trust me with a sharp blade. "Work here. I don't want you in my way in the kitchen."

Lola was separating egg whites from the yolks when I brought the peeled bulbs to the kitchen. With the glass bowl tilted at an angle, she worked her magic, beating the egg whites relentlessly with a fork until the glob expanded to a heaping bowlful. She transformed the shapeless goo into stiff foam with the same unbridled compulsion she employed to mete out discipline to form us into better shapes of ourselves.

The smell of aromatics sautéing in a glug of Baguio Oil danced in the air. In addition to minced beef, pork and shrimp, Lola packed her torta with an assortment of veggies. She emphasized the benefits of eating right. Injecting as many vitamins and minerals as she could into the well-liked dish was her clever way of balancing our diet. Adding extra vegetables was also a flavorsome and economical way of extending meals that were not being cooked just for us, but also for my two aunts and their families who lived outside the city.

On schooldays, while three of my cousins, my two sisters and I sat at our table for lunch, I'd pray that Mom, who worked abroad, would win the sweepstakes so she could return home to us. Sensing, for as long as I remember, the dagger of sorrow Daddy's passing had thrust into Mom's heart, I'd also pray that when the time came for anyone else in the family to go, the Lord would take us all at once, so everyone was spared the agony of grief. A fervent believer in the power of prayer, I spent more time praying than partaking of the gifts from His bounty.

Meanwhile, on the table, the torta, golden and round, glowed like a halo. I was still deep in prayer when my cousin Bob helped himself to a big slice. As he cut into it, a billow of steam and flecks of browned meat with shards of veggies escaped the omelet. I swallowed. I could almost taste it: savory with a hint of sweetness, soft yet springy against the coarseness of its stuffing.

Bob reached for a bottle of banana catsup and squeezed a generous dollop onto his plate. By then, the aroma of caramelized meat and veg was as tempting as sin. I sped up my prayers, worried that I might not get my fair share.

Lola carried on sweating over the stove as we ate. She performed her own miracle of feeding the multitude, packing her love in Tupperware boxes to send over to her two other daughters and their families.

Yes, Lola's torta sure stirs up a flood of recollections — all to be remembered with love, not shame, full of flavor but without bitterness.

Meatless Tortang Giniling
Lentil and Shrimp Omelet

You can add practically anything to your torta (omelet), but the more popular and traditional additions are giniling (minced meat), talong (eggplant) and alimango (crab). Diversity of ingredients is key to nutritional balance, and a way of making sure we get all the micronutrients our bodies need. Tortas are a clever way of introducing a broad spectrum of ingredients to our diet, and this torta recipe is packed with nutrient-rich vegetables. The usual minced meat (don't we get enough of it from burgers anyway?) is replaced with lentils — a nutrient powerhouse that supports heart health.

PREPARATION TIME
30 minutes + 10 minutes baking time
YIELD 6 servings

2 tablespoons olive oil
8 Guisa Ice Cubes, thawed (see page 17)
1 red bell pepper, seeded and diced small
8 oz (250 g) peeled, deveined raw shrimp, finely chopped
6 chestnut mushrooms, diced small
14-oz (400 g) can or 2 cups cooked lentils (rinsed well and drained)
6-oz (200 g) bag baby spinach
6 large eggs
⅓ teaspoon fine salt
⅓ teaspoon freshly ground pepper

PER SERVING CALORIES 286KCAL
FATS 12.6G | **SATURATED FAT** 2.3G
PROTEIN 20.4G
CARBOHYDRATES 27.4G
FIBER 8.8G | **SODIUM** 309MG
SUGARS 3.01G

1 Preheat the oven to 390°F (200°C). Lightly grease a 2-quart (1.9 L) baking dish (11 x 7 inches [28 x 18 cm]).
2 Heat a skillet over medium heat. Add the oil. When the oil shimmers, add the Guisa Ice Cubes and stir until completely melted.
3 Turn up the heat to high. Add the bell pepper. Cook, stirring occasionally for 2 minutes, until it starts to caramelize.
4 Add the shrimp and stir until slightly orange in color. Add the mushrooms and stir occasionally for 2 minutes or until they are browned. Add the lentils and stir for about 3 minutes until well combined. Add the spinach. Switch the heat off and stir until well combined. Transfer the contents of the skillet to the greased baking dish and spread evenly.
5 Crack the eggs into a bowl. Season with the salt and pepper. Beat thoroughly until blended.
6 Pour the eggs all over the mixture in the baking dish. Tilt the dish to ensure the egg is evenly spread. Place in the oven for about 10 minutes, until the egg has set. Remove from the oven and leave to cool. Cut into 6 equal portions.
7 Pack a serving of torta with rice or in a wholemeal Vegan Ube Pandesal (page 42) with lettuce, tomato and Banana Ketchup (page 42), and a side of fresh fruits. Refrigerate (keeps for about 3 days) or freeze the rest.

Freezing
Place cooled torta portions in a freezer-safe bag. Label and freeze (will keep for at least 1 month).

Reheating
Pop in the microwave at low heat for 1 minute or until warm.

Banana Ketchup

This staple condiment in Philippine households is said to have been invented by Filipina food scientist and World War II hero, Maria Orosa, using native bananas as the main ingredient. It's easy to make; this version uses a medley of fruit and vegetables, rather than sugar, to lend sweetness.

PREPARATION TIME 40 minutes
YIELD 1 cup

1 large banana (very ripe), chopped
¼ red onion, chopped
4 teaspoons tomato paste
¼ cup (50 g) dried apricots
8 pitted dates, chopped
⅓ cup (80 ml) coconut or cane vinegar
½ teaspoon garlic powder
3 slices pickled red beets, drained
½ teaspoon salt

1 Place all the ingredients, except the salt, in a blender and puree. Transfer to a saucepan on medium-high heat until it simmers. Lower the heat to medium-low and add the salt. Mix. Cover and allow to simmer for 30 minutes stirring frequently. If the mixture dries up, add a little water to achieve desired consistency.
2 Pour the mixture into a sterilized jar with a lid and allow to cool.
3 Place in the refrigerator. Use within 1 month.

PER SERVING **CALORIES** 20KCAL | **FATS** 0.1G
SATURATED FAT 0.01G | **PROTEIN** 0.27G
CARBOHYDRATES 5G | **FIBER** 0.6G
SODIUM 84MG **SUGARS** 3.4G

Vegan Ube Pandesal
Wholemeal Purple Yam Bread Rolls

Pandesal, from the Spanish words for "salt bread," is the bread of choice for the predominantly rice-eating Filipinos. It may have been born from the Spanish colonizers' attempts to make a European-style baguette.

PREPARATION TIME 2.5 hours
YIELD 20 bread rolls

3 cups (390 g) wholemeal bread flour soaked overnight in 2¼ cups (540 ml) warm water
½ cup (165 g) thawed grated ube purple yam or mashed boiled sweet potato
½ cup (120 ml) extra virgin olive oil + a few drops for coating the dough
3 cups (360 g) bread flour + a few tablespoons for kneading
2½ teaspoons instant yeast
¼ cup (40 g) coconut sugar
1 teaspoon salt
1 tablespoon chia seeds
2 tablespoons breadcrumbs

1 Mix the soaked wholemeal flour, purple yam or sweet potato and the ½ cup olive oil until well blended. Set aside.
2 In a large mixing bowl, add the bread flour, yeast, sugar, salt and chia seeds. Whisk together with a spatula or wooden spoon then push the dry ingredients against the sides of the bowl to make a well. Pour the wholemeal flour mixture into the center. Mix the dry flour and the wet flour gradually, drawing the flour from the inside walls of the well until well blended. (If you have a stand mixer you can use this to mix and knead the dough.)
3 Dust a clean, flat working surface with flour. Knead the dough on the floured surface with your hand until smooth, supple and elastic, about 10 minutes. Form into a ball and lightly coat with oil. Cover

with a damp towel or plastic wrap and let sit in a warm place (e.g., in an oven warmed for one minute then switched off) until the dough has doubled in volume, about 1 hour.

4 Punch the dough to let air out. Transfer onto a lightly floured surface or silicone mat and form into a donut. Divide into 4 equal pieces using a dough slicer or a knife. Straighten each piece and cut each into 5 equal portions. Shape each portion into a ball and place on a baking pan lined with parchment paper or a silicone baking mat. Make sure to leave a 1-inch (2.5 cm) gap in between each piece. Dust the rolls with the breadcrumbs. Cover the rolls with a damp cloth and leave to rise until doubled in volume, about 20 minutes.

5 Preheat the oven to 375°F (190°C).

6 Bake the rolls until golden, about 15 minutes. Serve and freeze the rest.

Freezing Freeze cooled pandesal in freezer bags. They will last for at least 1 month.

Reheating Thaw and reheat for a minute or two in the oven toaster.

This pandesal is given a healthier spin by using ube (purple yam) or kamote (sweet potato), wholemeal flour, chia seeds, coconut sugar instead of refined cane sugar, and olive oil instead of butter. The potassium-rich kamote was a staple in the diet of ancient Filipino tribes when rice was scarce, usually during the dry season. It was survival food for many Filipinos during World War II.

PER ROLL CALORIES 156KCAL | FATS 6.2G
SATURATED FAT 0.5G | PROTEIN 3.4G
CARBOHYDRATES 21.6G | FIBER 1G
SODIUM 152MG | SUGARS 2.7G

Precious Cargo

Liren Baker

Liren Baker is the author of the plant-forward cookbook *Meat to the Side* and she shares stories of the culinary world in her Kitchen Confidante blog and podcast. Her writing has been honored with a Legacy of Julia Child Award from the IACP (International Association of Culinary Professionals).

> *"Tita Leah was the keeper of secrets, the one [...] who knew how to cook, and she knew exactly how to make Grandma's recipes come back to life."*

Warmth radiated from my carry-on as I carefully placed it in the overhead locker. "Just don't tip over, it's a short flight," I thought, snapping the locker shut, and then settling into my seat and strapping myself in for the journey to Chicago.

It was the end of a quick trip back to New York for the holidays and as the plane took off into the frosty night, I thought of my dad and brother and sister, along with the entire clan of relatives from my mother's side. Our holiday gatherings were always so festive, and ever so delicious. The highlight was my aunt Tita Leah's cooking, her many hours in the kitchen fueling the magic of our gatherings.

Tita Leah was the keeper of secrets, the one who was blessed with my grandma's cooking genes. As much as my mom loved to bake, it was Tita Leah who knew how to cook and she knew exactly how to make my grandma's recipes come back to life after she passed away from cancer when I was twelve years old.

Cancer struck our family again years later, this time taking my mom, leaving a gaping hole in our hearts. I was eighteen and home from college that summer. Tita Leah, her husband and her two little ones moved into our house to see us through those first few months of bereavement, filling that hole with Tito Noli's jokes, giggling cousins and all the freshly cooked love that Tita Leah could serve.

Tita Leah taught me to cook and I would shadow her in the kitchen, peppering her with

> *"He fell in love. With me, yes, but also with Tita Leah's pancit bihon. And after we got married and built our life together in California, it was her recipe that would help us celebrate birthdays and holidays, year after year after year."*

questions, preparing myself to accept that she and her family couldn't stay with us forever. And that once I was done with college and started my career back home in New York, I would be the one at the stove, cooking for my dad and my very young brother and sister. I needed to learn, and I did, with her guidance along the way.

Tita Leah was the one who brought me my first kawali wok with a matching sandok ladle, the ultimate pasalubong homecoming gift, in the balikbayan box that she unpacked after a summer visit home to the Philippines. There, nestled amongst the candies and snacks that would temporarily extend a taste of home, was the cooking vessel that I would cherish most, with its hand-hammered metal and the promise of years of cooking ahead.

When I moved to the Midwest for graduate school, Tita Leah was on speed dial. If I needed to know how to make lumpiang shanghai for a party with friends, or what kind of noodles I should buy when I made the trek to the Filipino store in northern Chicago, I would call.

But nothing was better than being home to eat her cooking, especially her pancit bihon noodles, with the pata (pork leg) broth she simmered for hours, making it unquestionably the best. It was this pancit that she wrapped up for me to bring back to Chicago.

I knew that I needed to share this pancit with my then-boyfriend (now husband), Thomas. It was this precious cargo that I eagerly brought over to his apartment, straight from O'Hare Airport.

He fell in love. With me, yes, but also with Tita Leah's pancit bihon. And after we got married and built our life together in California, it was her recipe that would help us celebrate birthdays and holidays, year after year after year, all cooked in the kawali that I carried from New York to Chicago and finally, to California.

And then things changed. Thomas' cholesterol readings urged a health overhaul, spurring him to embrace a vegan diet. When his first birthday since his diet change came around, I was determined that there would still be pancit bihon.

My Vegetarian Pancit Bihon Guisado recipe was born out of necessity — and love — and I realized that in cooking this dish I could still find flavor, by making my own vegetarian fish sauce and embracing the umami of mushrooms. Cooking this dish reminds me that we must always find ways to keep memories and flavors alive, with whatever deck life has dealt us. And that in the end, life always manages to be delicious.

Vegetarian Pancit Bihon Guisado
Stir-Fried Rice Noodles

This pancit noodle dish is a beloved fiesta favorite with an all-veggie twist. The beauty of this dish is that it allows the vegetables to shine. Without any meat, it cooks faster, making it perfect for a packed lunch or weeknight meal.

PREPARATION TIME 30 minutes
YIELD 8 servings

4 cups (960 ml) low-sodium vegetable stock, or 1½ tablespoons Pinoy Powder (page 15) mixed with 4 cups hot water
8 oz (225 g) bihon noodles
2 tablespoons canola oil
3 cloves garlic, crushed
1 medium onion, finely diced
1 lb (500 g) trumpet mushrooms, sliced into bite-sized pieces
6 oz (200 g) firm tofu drained, dried and cut into ½-inch (1 cm) cubes
3 tablespoons low sodium soy sauce or coconut aminos
4 teaspoons vegetarian fish sauce or regular fish sauce
Ground pepper, to taste
2 carrots, cut into fine strips
2 celery stalks, sliced on the bias
1 Chinese/napa cabbage sliced
1 cup (100 g) snow peas
Cilantro, for garnish
8 calamansi or 2 lemons cut into wedges for garnish

1 Bring the stock to a boil in a large pot. Add the noodles to the boiling stock and cook for about 3 minutes. Drain, reserving the stock, and set aside both stock and noodles.

2 Heat the oil in a large wok over medium-high heat until it shimmers. Add the garlic and onion, stirring. When the onion is transparent, add the mushrooms and tofu. Stir till the tofu is slightly golden. Add the soy sauce, fish sauce and pepper.

3 Add the carrots, celery and cabbage. Turn the heat up to high, stirring occasionally. Add a bit of the reserved stock to avoid sticking. After about 2 minutes, when the vegetables are crisp yet tender, add the snow peas, noodles and the stock one cup at a time, taking care to not let the noodles get too soggy. Stir until well combined.

4 Serve garnished with cilantro and calamansi pieces or lemon wedges, for squeezing. Pack with a side of fresh fruits.

PER SERVING CALORIES 242KCAL
FATS 8.6G | SATURATED FAT 0.7G
PROTEIN 9.5G
CARBOHYDRATES 34.5G
FIBER 3.9G | SODIUM 548MG
SUGARS 3.1G

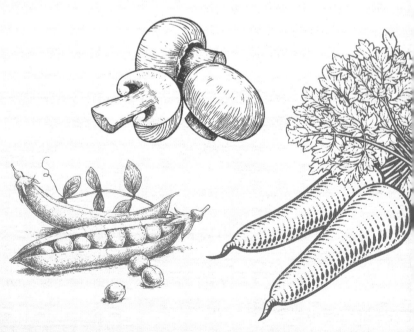

OPTION
If you have Guisa Ice Cubes (page 17) ready, you can swap garlic, onions and 1 teaspoon of fish sauce for 4 guisa cubes.

Back to Life

Ganthel Vergara

Ganthel Vergara is chef, owner and founder of ATO's Sisig & Grill, a Filipino Food truck in Richmond, Virginia, which he runs with the support of his wife Anne. He received his culinary training at Portland's Culinary Workshop in 2017. Ganthel worked as a paramedic before veering completely into food.

"Cooking is my first love. From the age of eight, I learned to cook in Lola's restaurant kitchen and learned the business side by spending time with her at the till."

My paramedic partner and I leapt up the flights of steps of a very narrow staircase in response to an emergency call. A seventy-year-old male had dialed in complaining of chest pain and difficulty in breathing. Though conscious and coherent when we arrived, the man was panting. His skin was ashen and upon examination we found his pulse weak and irregular. I clamped a pulse oximeter on his finger to measure the amount of oxygen in his blood. When I turned around to adjust the flow rate of his oxygen mask, the man toppled over and turned bluish. He stopped breathing. We checked his pulse. Nothing. Immediately, we set up an IV line, opened the defibrillator pack and cut open the unconscious man's shirt. Paddles in hand, the defib voice prompt counted, "Three, two, one!" An electric shock shook the man's body. No response. My partner pushed the heels of his palms on the man's chest repeatedly. "Give breath. Give breath," advised the voice prompt. Still no signs of revival. Press. Press. Press ... Another shock. Finally, his heart started beating. He was lucky: the rate for surviving cardiac arrest can be as low as one in fourteen.

My grandmother, Lola Helen, at the age of sixty-seven, wasn't as fortunate.

Lola Helen ran a family restaurant in Pasig, Metro Manila for thirty-seven years. It stood on the ground floor of a three-story building that housed my lola and lolo on the top floor and the restaurant staff on the second. My dad, my mom, my two sisters Michelle and Jennifer and I lived close to Lola's and visited at weekends.

> **"Several years into the job, the yearning to cook and operate a food business persisted. [...] Life is too short, I figured, to hold myself back from doing what I love."**

My favorite area was the kitchen. One of the restaurant's specialty dishes was the sisig pork hash. I loved to hear the sounds of the stock bubbling as the pork head boiled, the cleaver thumping on the wooden board as ingredients were minced, the oil spattering as garlic, ginger and onion were sautéed, and the sisig sizzling as it was ladled onto a hot plate. The kitchen buzzed with vitality.

Cooking is my first love. From the age of eight, I learned to cook in Lola's restaurant kitchen and I learned the business side by spending time with her at the till. Those times ended one morning in 1995 when Lola collapsed in the bathroom. Unfortunately, no paramedics were at the scene to revive her. Lola was rushed to the hospital, but because of the heavy traffic, she was gone on arrival. The restaurant didn't survive the heart attack either.

I'm not sure how much Lola's death had to do with my decision to train in the medical field instead of taking my chances in the culinary world. I'm sure, though, that the decision had a lot to do with the fact that I came from a family of health professionals. Dad is an orthopedic surgeon, Mom is a nurse and my sister Michelle is a pediatrician. As the only son, there was a tacit and rational expectation that I would follow in the family footsteps, rather than following my heart. A degree in saving lives guaranteed a rewarding job and food on the table. And so, I became a paramedic. When I moved to the US in 2009, I continued my medical career, earning an EMT- Paramedic associate degree in Portland, Oregon. I worked for almost three years in the Pacific Northwest.

I had no regrets. However, several years into the job, the yearning to cook and operate a food business persisted. Like plaques in the arteries, my pent-up love for cooking restricted joy from flowing to my heart and begged to be resuscitated. Life is too short, I figured, to hold myself back from doing what I love.

✳ ✳ ✳

In 2018, I moved from Portland to Richmond and started up a food truck. I named it ATO's, an acronym for the names of my kids: Alex, Tomas and Ondrea. I've retired from my medical practice and decided to bring myself and hopefully, the people I cook for to life, so to speak, through food. As Mark Twain said, I believe that "you will be more disappointed by the things you didn't do than by the ones you did do."

Inasal Sisig Grilled Chicken Hash

A heart-healthy spin on the indulgent dish of sisig pork hash, this version uses chicken. Have it one way by making grilled chicken inasal only or sisig only (you can use ready-grilled chicken if you're cutting back on calories or strapped for time). Have it both ways if you're not!

PREPARATION TIME 1 hour + at least
  2 hours marinating time
YIELD 6 servings

"Inasal" means "barbecue" in Hiligaynon or Ilonggo, one of the languages spoken in the Visayan region. It has become known all over the Philippines as the name for a special kind of charcoal-roasted chicken originating from the city of Bacolod, regarded as the country's chicken capital. The marinade made with annatto oil, and the smoky flavor from placing the meat high above the heat, differentiates inasal from other kinds of skewered grills.

HOW TO MAKE ANNATTO OIL

Heat a small pan over medium heat. Pour in 3 tablespoons of oil. When the oil shimmers, add 1 tablespoon of annatto seeds. Stir. When the color of the oil turns bright orange, remove from the heat. Strain and discard the seeds. You can substitute annatto oil with beetroot powder, which can be bought at health food stores.

PER SERVING CALORIES 510KCAL
FATS 20.07G | SATURATED FAT 3.3G
PROTEIN 41.88G | CARBOHYDRATES 38.6G
FIBER 3G | SODIUM 564MG | SUGARS 9.53G

CHICKEN INASAL
2 lbs (1 kg) skinless chicken breast or thigh
  fillets, thinly sliced

MARINADE
½ cup (120 ml) coconut or apple cider vinegar
1 tablespoon coconut aminos
½ cup (120 ml) mango juice or orange juice
  (pure juice, not from concentrate)
¼ cup (60 ml) calamansi or lime juice
2 stalks lemongrass, chopped
1 tablespoon minced ginger
1 tablespoon minced garlic
1 teaspoon garlic powder
1 tablespoon brown or coconut sugar
1 bay leaf
½ teaspoon salt
½ teaspoon ground black pepper
3 tablespoons annatto oil (see below)

ASPARAGUS
1¼ lbs (700g) asparagus, trimmed
1 tablespoon sunflower oil
Pinch of sea salt

SISIG
2 tablespoons sunflower oil
1 medium yellow onion, diced
4 oz (120 g) chicken liver, chopped
1 medium red onion, diced
2 tablespoons coconut aminos
2 tablespoons light mayonnaise
1 red chili pepper, minced, optional
Pepper, to taste
Juice of 2 calamansi or ½ lime

Make the grilled chicken inasal

1 Mix the marinade ingredients in a bowl until well combined.
2 Place chicken in a ziplock bag. Pour the marinade into the bag and make sure all the chicken is in contact with the marinade. Let the air out of the bag and seal. Refrigerate and leave to marinate for at least 2–3 hours.
3 Prepare a charcoal grill. (Or you can use a stovetop grill pan or skillet, if you prefer.)
4 Drain the excess marinade from the chicken into a saucepan. Allow to simmer for at least 3 minutes. Use this mixture as the basting sauce. (If using a stovetop griddle or skillet, lightly grease and place over high heat.)
5 Grill the chicken on both sides, basting it generously and frequently. When the chicken's exterior is glazed with a caramelized char, remove from the heat. (If not proceeding with the sisig recipe, make sure the chicken is cooked through.) Do not discard the leftover basting sauce.

Make the asparagus

1 Coat the asparagus with the oil and sprinkle with the salt.
2 Grill for 2–4 minutes, until lightly charred and fork-tender, turning often to brown evenly.
3 Remove the asparagus from the grill and set aside until ready to serve.

Make the sisig hash

1 Chop the chicken inasal prepared earlier (or the equivalent amount of ready-grilled chicken breast) into fine pieces and set aside.
2 Heat a pan on medium-high heat. Add the oil and heat until it shimmers. Add the yellow onion and stir until soft. Add the chicken liver, crushing it, until fully cooked.

3 Add the chicken and the red onion and cook for about 5–10 minutes, until the onion has softened, stirring often. Add the coconut aminos, mayonnaise, excess basting sauce from the Chicken Inasal, and chili (if using) and mix for about 3 minutes until well blended. Add a pinch of pepper, to taste. Sprinkle with the calamansi or lime juice and mix.
4 Transfer to a serving plate or lunch box and serve with the asparagus and half a cup of plain rice per serving.
5 Alternatively, wrap in a banana leaf like the traditional binalot or pastil from the Mindanao region.

Oven-Baked Chicken And Chunky Fries

adapted by Jacqueline Chio-Lauri

Fried chicken was a favorite food in the Philippines long before fast-food giant Jollibee came along. But it was Jollibee that popularized Chickenjoy, their fried-chicken signature item, which is now a nationwide household name. The long hours Filipinos endure queuing up at new store openings of Jollibee in the US and Europe shows Jollibee's profound foothold in the appetite of Filipinos. Chickenjoy is a perfect example of how a dish (fried chicken) with foreign origin (US) has been indigenized, then glocalized (globalized and localized). This oven-baked copycat is adapted from a recipe by Doris Sømme, a caterer in Norway. It mimics the crunch of biting into deep-fried chicken and the juiciness and taste Filipinos so love about this universal comfort food.

PREPARATION TIME 30 minutes
  + overnight to marinate
  + 1.5 hours roasting time
YIELD 6 servings

MARINADE
1 tablespoon Pinoy Powder (page 15)
½ teaspoon paprika
1 tablespoon extra-virgin olive oil
2 teaspoons coconut aminos
¼ teaspoon calamansi
  or lemon juice

OVEN-BAKED CHICKEN
6 chicken drumsticks, about 1 lb (500g) total
2 tablespoons olive oil, divided
1 tablespoon all-purpose flour, or ½ tablespoon cornstarch + ½ tablespoon rice flour
1 teaspoon Pinoy Powder (page 15)
1 egg
1¼ cups panko breadcrumbs

PER SERVING CALORIES 494KCAL
FATS 26.5G | SATURATED FAT 5.5G
PROTEIN 29.8G
CARBOHYDRATES 61.4G | FIBER 9.2G
SODIUM 474MG | SUGARS 6.2G

1 Combine the marinade ingredients in a large bowl. Add the chicken drumsticks and toss, making sure each drumstick is well coated with marinade. Cover and place overnight in the refrigerator.

2 Preheat the oven to 400°F (200°C).

3 Lightly grease a wire rack with 1 tablespoon of the olive oil, using a paper towel or brush. Set aside. Line a baking sheet with parchment paper.

4 In a bowl, combine the flour and Pinoy Powder. In another bowl, whisk the egg and remaining 1 tablespoon of olive oil with a fork. Pour little by little into the flour and Pinoy Powder and mix until you have a smooth and well-blended batter.

5 Place the panko breadcrumbs in another bowl.

6 Add the drumsticks to the batter and mix to coat evenly. Dredge each drumstick in the panko breadcrumbs and place on the lined baking sheet so that they don't touch each other.

7 Roast in the preheated oven for 25–30 minutes or until the top sides turn golden.

8 Take out of the oven and use tongs to carefully transfer each drumstick to a wire rack with the uncooked side up. Keep at least a ½ inch (1 cm) space between each drumstick. Place the wire rack on the baking sheet and return to the oven. Bake for another 25–30 minutes until done or until the meat has begun to shrink away from the bone. The drumsticks should reach an internal temperature of 180°F (82°C).

MAKE-AHEAD TIP

Store the cooled roasted vegetables in a resealable container in the refrigerator for up to 5 days. Alternatively, freeze in ziplock bags or freeze-safe containers for up to 2 months. Thaw overnight in the refrigerator. Reheat in the microwave for about 1–2 minutes before eating.

Refrigerating or freezing

Let the drumsticks cool to room temperature. Wrap individually in foil and place all together in a zip-top bag. Refrigerate (if using the following day) or freeze (for up to 2 weeks).

Reheating from the refrigerator

Take the chicken out of the refrigerator. Preheat the oven to 350°F (175°C). Open the foil-wrapped chicken. Place on an oven-safe sheet with the foil wrapper as an under liner. Pop in the preheated oven for 10–15 minutes, in the center rack, for an even application of heat.

Reheat from frozen

Same as reheating from the refrigerator but allow more time for the chicken to thaw before placing in the oven.

Keeping chicken crispy in lunch boxes

Make sure there's air space in the lunch box to avoid steaming that would make the crispy coating soggy. Place the chicken on top of folded paper towels when packing to absorb moisture. Don't forget to pack fresh fruit with the lunch boxes!

CHUNKY FRIES

3 medium potatoes, quartered then quartered again lengthwise, to make 16 wedges

3 large carrots, halved crosswise and quartered lengthwise

3 large zucchini, halved crosswise and quartered lengthwise

3 tablespoons olive oil

2 tablespoons Pinoy Powder (page 15)

1 Turn the oven temperature to 425°F (220°C). Place the potatoes, carrots and zucchini on a baking sheet lined with a silicone baking mat or parchment paper. Pour the olive oil and sprinkle the Pinoy Powder over the veggies and mix to coat evenly. Set aside the zucchini on another lined baking sheet.

2 Arrange the potatoes and carrots on the lined baking sheet making sure the pieces don't touch each other.

3 Place in the oven for about 20–25 minutes or until fork tender and caramelized on the edges.

4 Place the zucchini in the oven for about 10 minutes or until fork tender and caramelized on the edges.

CHAPTER 3

Pulutan, Sabaw at Merienda

Nibbles, Soups and Noshes

Filipino meals are traditionally one-course affairs. Dishes are served all at once and eaten at the same time. We do, however, have appetizers or small tapas-like nibbles called pulutan, eaten with drinks. Sabaw (soups) tend to be hearty meals on their own, but if you are looking for a light first course to whet the appetite and aid digestion, try the delicious recipe for Sinigang sa Calamansi (Sour and Savory Soup) by Michelin-starred chef Roger Joya on page 68 of this chapter. It will also fill you up, reducing the urge to stoke up on the main course. Aside from breakfast, lunch and dinner, we like noshing on merienda (snacks) in between — we can get away with this as main meals rarely include starters and desserts. This chapter showcases some of the biggest names in Filipino cooking — adobo, sinigang and lumpia — in smaller bites.

Recipes in this chapter are closely in line with the 2019 American Heart Health program, which recommends that appetizers and soups should contain no more than 240 mg of sodium, 250 calories and 2 teaspoons of added sugars per serving.

Sour and Savory

Margarita Manzke

Philippine-born and raised Margarita Manzke, with multiple James Beard Award nominations, received degrees from Le Cordon Bleu in London and the Culinary Institute of America in New York, before moving to Los Angeles. In 2017, she opened Sari Sari Store, a Filipino restaurant in the Los Angeles Grand Central Market.

"I was the kind of gal who spent her summers plotting how to augment her meager school allowance and working."

Long gone were the days when French restaurants employed an extensive kitchen brigade and when responsibilities were delegated to different individuals who specialized in certain tasks: when only certificat d'aptitude professionnelle (CAP)–trained charcutiers could cure meats, only sauciers could prepare sauces, stews and sautés, and only boulangers baked breads. That was far from my reality when we opened a fifty-seater French bistro on California's Monterey Peninsula in 2002. At our ambitious restaurant where everything — including pasta, bread, pastries, chocolate and ice cream — was made by us from scratch, what choice did I have? I was in charge of overseeing the kitchen team, but what's to oversee when we didn't have enough staff to man every station? I faced two options: run away as fast as I could and never return, or roll up my sleeves, woman up, and get down to work, which also meant waving goodbye to life outside of that kitchen.

It gave me a sense of déjà vu. I grew up in the Philippines spending most of my summers at the beach, where the sand was as pale as French crêpe batter. My parents ran a bayside resort, but if you think I was the type who'd pass her days frolicking on the shore or lounging on a shaded sunbed sipping chilled buko juice out of a fresh coconut — you don't know me at all. I was the kind of gal who spent her summers plotting how to augment her meager school allowance and working. I'd be found either in

> **"Life without striking a balance between work and play would be like adobo devoid of either sourness or savor. [...] The way one enhances the other [...] is the recipe for a more sumptuous life."**

the kitchen scooping rice onto plates that went out to big banquets held at the resort, or on the beach setting up stall to sell food to passersby. One summer, a business idea bloomed in my head. I talked my father into lending me money. I needed the capital to buy pigs and to pay a man to slaughter, bamboo skewer and roast the hogs over coals until their skins crisped and bronzed. Once cooked, I'd plate the chopped-up lechon roasted pig and sell it on the beach with a dollop of brown sweet and sour sauce made of liver, vinegar and sugar.

My childhood predilection for industry followed me into adulthood. In the cramped little kitchen of our newly opened French bistro, while dough for the day's freshly baked bread was being kneaded in a tiny mixer that had seen better days, I'd rush to the dessert station, douse the work table with flour and spread out pastry dough with a rolling pin. While the soupe à l'oignon simmered in stock to develop deep flavor, I stirred roux for the sauces I still needed to make in a pan. After whisking egg whites into a consommé over the stove, I jumped to the cold section to trim artichoke hearts as fast as I could to make it back in time to the consommé before it bubbled. That was my life — fifteen hours a day, six days a week.

Amid endless periods of preparing elaborate dishes of a cuisine that wasn't originally my own, I found solace in cooking adobo, with its two key ingredients, vinegar and soy sauce. Vinegar provides balance and amplifies flavors (and lends

mouth-puckering goodness); soy sauce, with its saltiness and umami we Filipinos call linamnam, tempers sourness — without which adobo could fall flat and lifeless.

Before the restaurant would open, I'd gather the staff and share with them this simple dish that grounds me to my roots. A whiff of the braised chicken and pork glistening with sauce would still hang in the air as we ate. Its taste — the right blend of tartness and saltiness — gave this food identity, character and life.

※ ※ ※

I reaped the rewards of my hard work. I moved forward to open several more restaurants, including my own, since my stint at the French Bistro in Monterey. Nevertheless, life, I now reflect in hindsight, is like a plate of adobo. For life without striking a balance between work and play would be like adobo devoid of either sourness or savor. Yes, the dish would still be edible without the counteracting interchange between these two tastes, but their balanced coexistence, the way one enhances the other, I shall keep reminding myself, is the recipe for a more sumptuous life.

Shishito Pepper Adobo

Adobo is an indigenous way of cooking or braising food with vinegar, and great for cooking proteins or vegetables. This recipe, adapted from Chef Margarita's Sari-Sari Store pulutan (appetizer) menu, features shishito peppers, rich in vitamin C and antioxidants. Crisp shards of fried garlic spiked with chili add texture and zing to the tangy, sweet and salty flavors. This recipe also works well with sliced bell pepper instead of shishito.

TYPE OF DISH Pulutan
   (appetizer)
PREPARATION TIME
   15 minutes
YIELD 4 servings

ADOBO SAUCE
1½ tablespoons white vinegar
2½ tablespoons coconut
   aminos
2 tablespoons water
½ onion, roughly chopped
1 tablespoon garlic, chopped
1 teaspoon black pepper,
   freshly ground
1 star anise
1 bay leaf

CHILI GARLIC (OPTIONAL)
½ teaspoon chili powder
¼ cup calamansi or lemon juice
1 teaspoon garlic powder

FRIED GARLIC
2 tablespoons olive oil
1 head garlic, sliced

GRILLED SHISHITO
24 shishito peppers
Pinch of rock salt

CALORIES 119KCAL | **FATS** 7G
SATURATED FAT 1G **PROTEIN** 1.9G
CARBOHYDRATES 13.6G
FIBER 2.25G | **SODIUM** 225.5MG
SUGARS 5.7G

1 Place all the adobo sauce ingredients in a small saucepan over medium-high heat. Bring to a boil then turn down the heat to medium low. Simmer for about 3 minutes until the onion is translucent. Remove from the heat. Take out the star anise and bay leaf and discard. Let cool.

2 For the Chili Garlic, mix all the ingredients in a bowl and set aside.

3 For the Fried Garlic, heat the oil in a skillet over medium heat until it shimmers. Add the garlic and stir-fry until golden. Remove the fried garlic from the skillet with a slotted spoon. Transfer and drain on paper towels. Set aside.

4 Cook the shishito. Use the same skillet used for frying the garlic. Turn the heat to high. Put in the shishito peppers in a single layer and sear. Once one side is blistered, about 3 minutes, turn each pepper over until the other side is also blistered. Place in a serving bowl.

5 Pour the adobo sauce over the peppers and mix until completely coated. Pour in the chili garlic mixture if using and stir. Top with the fried garlic and a pinch of rock salt before serving.

Cita's Recipe for Lumpia

Meshelle Armstrong

Meshelle Armstrong is the co-owner of Kaliwa Restaurant in Washington DC. She is also the ringmistress behind the Eat Good Food Group of restaurants, partner of Irish chef Cathal Armstrong and the tiger mama of Eve and Eamonn.

> *"Even though finances were tight, Mom made sure I attended a good school. 'You hab to hab da best education,' she'd say. [...] She worked two jobs to make sure of it."*

I grew up in the eighties, a Filipino-American girl raised by a single mom. We had little money, but my mom, Cita, made up for it with her rich personality. She was proud of her heritage. Her family "back home in da Philippines," she'd say in her accent, were affluent and cultured.

Even though finances were tight, Mom made sure I attended a good school. "You hab to hab da best education," she'd say. (Like many first-generation Filipinos, she tended to mix up her f's and p's and her v's and b's, something I teased and tormented her about over the years.) She worked two jobs to make sure of it. As she ran from job to job, I waited at friends' houses for her to collect me. When we reached home, our evening meals were usually TV dinners — you know, those square tin trays with little compartments for meat, veggies and sometimes even dessert? I remember wishing Mom could cook like my friends' moms did. But my mom couldn't cook a thing, or so I thought.

When Filipinos get together for a party, it's a food fest and you'd better bring it. Once, Mom was asked to make lumpia, specifically lumpiang shanghai, a skinny close relative of the egg roll. It's usually filled with meat, rolled tightly into the size of a finger in a flimsy flour-based wrapper, then fried until crunchy and golden brown. Though a staple at Filipino gatherings, everyone concocts their own assortment of fillings and prepares lumpia their own way. As for Mom, I was sure she'd order it from the local turo-turo (an

> **"I learned that day that lumpia making was not only a detailed process or a ritual of sorts, it was also an occasion to instill family values. I learned a lesson I would carry my whole life."**

eatery where you "point-point" to what you want) and pass it off as hers. She didn't.

Helping her unpack the grocery bags, real food spilled out: fresh carrots, scallions, eggs, pork butchered by a guy who wore an apron, and shrimp straight from the DC Wharf pier. Mom took on a different air as she methodically separated the thin lumpia wrappers from each other. She appeared to know what she was doing! Reluctantly, she handed me a batch. I ripped the first few. Mom glared at me — I knew what she was thinking, "Don't waste!" So, I took extra care in pulling the rest apart gently.

Mom moved on to preparing the mixture. "Make sure the lumpia filling is 'playborful,'" she said. "Don't rely on the sukka," referring to the sawsawan or dip-dip sauce of vinegar and spices that accompany lumpia. Filipinos like to dunk food in seasonings or dipping sauces ranging from trickles to torrents depending on taste and preference.

Using her hands, Mom combined all the ingredients in a bowl. She added eggs to the mix to bind the filling ingredients together. Then came the more challenging part — rolling and wrapping what would be crispy bits of heaven. This part required dexterity and precision: too tight and the roll might burst open, too loose and it might fall apart; too much filling and it might not cook all the way through, too little filling and it would lack oomph. To seal off the roll, the final pat-pat of water had to be just right too. Ahhh, the pressure!

What made Mom's lumpia different had nothing to do with flavor or ingredients; it had more to do with technique and tenacity. Most people would buy ready-minced pork or use a grinder or a food processor to finely chop the meat. Not Mom. Mom used a sharp knife and lots of elbow grease. Her swan-like neck tensely bent, she chop-chop-chopped and chop-chop-chopped until the pork and shrimp were perfectly hashed. She exuded fierceness, the shimmering blade of steel like an extension of her own hand.

I was exhausted just watching her. "Mooooom, why didn't you just use the grinder!?" She looked up at me in a way she had never did and said, enunciating each consonant clearly, "Don't. E-ver. Be. Lazy!"

I learned that day that making lumpia was not only a detailed process or a ritual of sorts, it was also an occasion to instill family values. I learned lessons I would carry my whole life.

At the end of the party, after everyone had left, we lovingly laughed about my cousins and titas (aunts) while cleaning up. Both of us knew — Mom had not just passed on a recipe for lumpia to me, she had passed on a rite.

Lumpiang Shanghai
Shrimp and Pork Egg Rolls

Long ago, deep-frying was a luxury only enjoyed by the elite, as it required a metal pot (rare in the olden days) and lots of oil and wood. Today, lumpiang shanghai is one of the most celebrated dishes among Filipinos worldwide. Meshelle achieves the delightful crunch this dish is known for without deep-frying in this recipe adapted from her mom's.

TYPE OF DISH Pulutan
  (appetizer)
PREPARATION TIME 1 hour
YIELD about 50 rolls or 15
  appetizer servings

1 medium size onion, finely
  chopped
1 large carrot, finely chopped
2 celery stalks, finely chopped
6 cloves garlic, minced
1 lb (500 g) shrimp, peeled and
  minced
1 lb (500 g) pork, 5% fat ratio,
  minced
1 egg, lightly beaten
2 tablespoons flour
3 tablespoons coconut aminos
½ teaspoon ground pepper
50 spring roll wrappers, each
  5 inches (12 cm) square

CHOPPING TIP
Chop the onion, carrot and celery roughly and place in a food processor with the garlic and shrimp. Pulse until finely chopped and well blended.

PER SERVING WITHOUT KETCHUP
CALORIES 175KCAL | FATS 5.6G
SATURATED FAT 1G
PROTEIN 14G | CHOLESTEROL 190MG
CARBOHYDRATES 16G | FIBER 0.8G
SODIUM 226MG | SUGARS 3.7G

1 In a large bowl, combine all the ingredients except the wrappers. Mix until well combined.
2 Pour a little water into a small bowl. Set aside. Lay one wrapper on a clean work surface so that it looks like a diamond. Scoop a tablespoon of meat mixture onto the center of the wrapper. Spread the mixture across, leaving about half an inch on both ends empty. Fold the bottom corners up and over the meat. Dip your fingers or a brush into the bowl of water and moisten the top corner of the wrapper to seal. Roll tightly all the way up. Repeat until all the mixture is rolled into the wrappers. (You can deep-freeze excess rolls in freezer-safe containers or bags without overlapping them. They will keep for at least 1 month.)
3 Preheat the oven to 425°F (220°C).
4 Arrange the rolls in a single layer on a baking sheet lined with a silicone baking mat or parchment paper.
5 Bake in the preheated oven for 10 minutes. Turn the rolls over carefully using a pair of tongs. Bake for another 7–8 minutes or until golden. Serve while warm and crunchy with Banana Ketchup (page 42).

Mastering the Art

Carlo Lamagna

Philippine-born and Detroit-raised Carlo Lamagna is the chef-owner of modern Filipino restaurant, Magna Kusina, in Portland, Oregon. A 2022 James Beard Award Best Chef finalist, the chef he most reveres is his late father, Willie, who, alongside his mother Gloria, is his inspiration.

"The martial arts [...] fascinated me and mastering arnis was one of the ways I had immersed myself into the culture of my birth country."

The sound of the click-clacking of sticks ricocheted around the hall. A woman, light on her feet, charged at me repeatedly. She wielded a two-foot rattan cane and thrust it at various angles at different parts of my body. Each time she struck, I met the blow with equal force, swinging a similar baton to parry the attack. The offense and defense went on for over a minute like a choreographed dance on time lapse, until one of us dropped our weapon.

Sparring was part of the routine training at my arnis class at the University of the Philippines, where I worked myself up from student to instructor. Arnis is the national martial arts of the Philippines, practiced by indigenous warriors since the precolonial era. By the time the Spanish fleet headed by Ferdinand Magellan landed on our shores in 1521, island natives were able to beat the hell out of the armored, musket-bearing invaders with far less sophisticated weaponry by using their superior arnis combat skills. The martial arts, steeped in history, fascinated me and mastering arnis was one of the ways I had immersed myself into the culture of my birth country.

My family had left the Philippines when I was a few months old. I grew up in Windsor, Canada and Detroit, USA before we returned to Manila when I was eleven. The transition back to the homeland was a culture shock. Though both my parents are Filipinos, it didn't prepare me for the Philippine way of life, mentality, attitude, customs and traditions. Moving back was like pushing open a

> ## "When I cook, I am transported back to the Philippines [...] The result is what my good friend and business partner calls 'old school flavors, new school style'."

high, solid gate that revealed an expansive terrain filled with twists and turns.

It was hard to navigate, alright. A hefty part of each day was spent commuting. Different forms of public transport overflowing with passengers, and countless private vehicles bobbed and weaved through the streets, making a one-mile journey last for ages. Walking or biking wasn't a good idea either — the heat was one reason and unsuitable infrastructure was another.

On my daily commute, I'd squeeze myself into jam-packed jeepneys, the flashy icons of the city's thoroughfares. I learned where to wait to flag one down and when and where to shout out "Para!" to get off. I became seasoned in passing fares to the driver and passing change back to passengers. Laminated with sweat as I waited under the sun for a jeepney, I'd often refresh myself at a samalamig (coolers) stand. Pulp, chunks of fruit or jello swam in clear plastic jars filled with multi-colored chilled beverages, such as sago't gulaman (sago pearls and agar), buko pandan (coconut infused with pandan flavor) and melon coolers. Calamansi (Philippine lime) juice was my regular pick. The vendor would scoop it with a ladle into a plastic cup.

Next to the stand, I'd protein-load with tokneneng, deep-fried boiled eggs in flaming orange-colored batter dunked in a heavenly spiced vinegar dip, called pinakurat. Paired with the calamansi juice, it hit all the right spots. Before long, enjoying jeepney rides was another art I had mastered.

Eventually, I adapted and thrived in my new environment. In a few months, I picked up the language. The more comfortable I became with the local tongue, the more confident I became in interacting with the locals. A few more years and I was totally in the groove. My appetite for adventure and my thirst for exploration deepened. Aside from arnis, my curiosity pivoted to food. No street food vendor was too iffy for me to try. The old woman sat on the corner of the street by the lamp post with a cloth-covered abaca basket dangling a bottle of spiced vinegar didn't escape my attention, even before she called, "Baluuut!" to advertise the fertilized duck eggs she was selling. Not far from the campus where I taught arnis, billows of smoke and an irresistible barbecue aroma led me to an isawan ("isaw" comes from the word "isawsaw" or "to dip"), a stall with nothing but a portable charcoal grill searing skewered chicken intestines and a makeshift table crammed with bottles of zestful dipping sauces. I knew some of the vendors by name. I got to know their life stories as much as I got to know their food.

These are the sights, sounds, smells, feelings and tastes I took with me when I moved back to the US and opened a restaurant. When I cook, I am transported back to the Philippines and I interpret my experiences on the plate. The result is what my good friend and business partner calls "old-school flavors, new-school style." It's another art form I've mastered. The art of being me.

Tokneneng-Inspired Eggs

Entrepreneurial flair allegedly gave birth to this Pinoy street food. The story goes that a food vendor, left with a lot of unsold balut (fertilized duck egg), invented a way to cut her losses. She dredged the shelled balut with flour, plopped them in the deep-fryer and sold them on sticks. Eventually, the recipe evolved to use regular boiled eggs and orange-colored batter tinted by annatto seeds. Its moniker was derived from the word for "egg" used in a Pinoy comic series in 1978 — tokneneng. Today, the snack is part of the country's daytime street-food scene, offering the masses a quick, cheap and freshly cooked hunger-stancher while on the fly. Carlo gives the tokneneng a healthier spin while keeping all its tasty dipping-sauce glory.

TYPE OF DISH Merienda (snack)
PREPARATION TIME 30 minutes
YIELD 1 cup (240 ml) of vinaigrette (good for 16 servings); 4 servings of salad

CALAMANSI VINAIGRETTE

¼ cup (60 ml) calamansi juice or lime juice
2 tablespoons orange juice
1 tablespoon orange zest
2 tablespoons fish sauce
¼ cup (85 g) honey
½ teaspoon chili flakes
½ cup (120 ml) grapeseed oil

Put the juices, zest, fish sauce, honey and chili flakes in a blender. Blend for about 20 seconds on medium. Turn the speed to low and slowly add the grapeseed oil until the mixture is emulsified. If the vinaigrette separates at any point, simply whisk back together or shake. Refrigerate until needed. This dressing keeps for up to 2 weeks in the refrigerator.

PER SERVING CALORIES 249.8KCAL
FATS 17.53G | **SATURATED FAT** 2G
PROTEIN 11.75G | **CARBOHYDRATES** 13.25G
FIBER 4.2G **SODIUM** 226MG | **SUGARS** 8.03G

TOKNENENG EGG SALAD

4 small eggs
1 head Little Gem romaine lettuce, lightly grilled, sliced (see tip, facing page)
½ cup (70 g) kohlrabi, cut into fine strips or broccoli, finely chopped
1 scallion, sliced on the bias
Pinch of salt
Pinch of freshly ground black pepper
1 tablespoon orange zest
½ tablespoon toasted sesame seeds

In a saucepan, boil enough water to submerge 4 eggs. Place the eggs carefully into the boiling water with a spoon. Lower the heat to a simmer and cook the eggs for 7 minutes. Prepare an ice bath while the eggs are cooking. Remove the eggs from the heat and immediately cool in the ice bath for at least 1 minute. Peel the eggs.

Serving the dish

Pour ¼ cup (60 ml) of the dressing into a mixing bowl and swirl to coat the sides of the bowl with the dressing. Add the lettuce, kohlrabi and scallion and gently fold them in. Lightly season with salt and pepper. Mix thoroughly. Divide between 4 plates. Nest a halved egg on top of each salad serving. Sprinkle with orange zest and toasted sesame seeds.

TIP

To grill a lettuce, slice it in half and lightly brush all sides with a little oil. Place cut sides down on a griddle over medium-high heat for about a minute or until seared. Flip and grill for another minute.

Michelin Star

Roger Asakil Joya

At age seventeen, Roger Asakil Joya emigrated from the Philippines to Norway. He is the chef and founder of Michelin-starred restaurant, Sabi Omakase. Besides being an award-winning sushi master, he is also the co-founder and co-owner of a popular chain of restaurants in Norway called Sabi Sushi.

> *Michael Ellis said [...] "Fill your place with happy diners and Michelin star recognition follows." I can't think of a place more deserving of a star than home.*

It's February 22, 2017 at a Michelin Guide awards ceremony in a grand theater in Stockholm. On stage, propped on stands and encircled by a spotlight are three familiar flower-shaped cut-outs — the star symbols awarded to restaurants for outstanding cooking that any chef would die for. A pile of tires, in honor of Michelin, the founding tire company that has been giving out these awards since 1900, sits next to the stands. Rouge drapes, the same hue as the cover of the annually awaited guide book that lists the best restaurants across the region, form the backdrop.

Lights dim. The event, attended by chefs, journalists and photographers, kicks off with the title "The Michelin Guide Nordic Countries" splashed on the projector screen. The Nordic edition of the Michelin Guide book, featuring recognized restaurants in Denmark, Finland, Iceland, Norway and Sweden, had included Stavanger in Norway, the city where my restaurant is located, for the first time last year, the year my business partner alerted me that "the Michelin Man" might dine at our omakase restaurant.

The bare bones of an omakase meal at our restaurant are no different from those of the meals I grew up eating: fish and rice. Raised on a rice plantation in Cavite on Manila Bay, sea-to-table and farm-to-table cooking were the orders of the day. My big family, with four brothers and four sisters, would sit at a round table facing each other in the same intimate and homely atmosphere I replicate in my 250-square-foot restaurant, Sabi Omakase. On the lazy Susan,

> **"The bare bones of an omakase meal at our restaurant are no different from those of the meals I grew up eating: fish and rice. Raised on a rice plantation [...] Sea-to-table and farm-to-table cooking were the orders of the day."**

my grandmother or mother would set before us nature's gifts of the day to share. There was always steamed rice; grains harvested from our field that I helped dry under the sun. There were other dishes, too, of course. If I had gone fishing and managed a good haul, fish sinigang, a soup soured with fruits and complemented with vegetables in season would accompany the rice. It wasn't much but it was plenty.

I wondered who the Michelin inspectors could be? In the movie *Burnt*, the Maître d' warns his staff, "No one knows who they are. No one. They come, they eat, they go, but . . ." — he pauses — "they have habits. The Michelin Man eats in pairs." "The Michelin Man can even be a woman," the hostess interjects. The Maître d' continues, "They always book a table before seven thirty. The first of the pair arrives early and has a drink at the bar. Their partner arrives half an hour later. One orders the tasting menu, the other one a la carte. Always."

Hmm . . . that wasn't much help to me. First, no one eats in pairs in my restaurant; diners eat together: a guest doesn't book a table; a guest books a seat — at the ten-seater L-shaped sushi counter. Everyone eats at the same time because it takes three and a half hours to complete the seventeen-course omakase experience. Lastly, nobody has a drink at the bar because there is no bar and no one orders from a menu because there isn't one; guests trust me, the oyakata chef, to choose for them, while the sommelier assists them in selecting wines to pair with the food.

The host, Swedish racing driver Ramona Carlsson, walks onstage. "Let's introduce the new stars of the Michelin Guide Nordic Countries 2017!"

The screen lights up showing a map of the Nordic region. To a soundtrack of slow, droning music with sudden crescendos, the flower-like star icon flies in on screen and zooms in on Norway. My heart flutters. The star lands on Stavanger.

"Please welcome on stage," Ramona announces, "the chef, Roger Asakil Joya from the restaurant Sabi Omakase from Stavanger, Norway! A big round of applause."

I walk on stage and signal to my team to follow me. The guide's director, Michael Ellis, hands me the red guide book and the Michelin trophy as my wife and colleague Anna, and sommelier Magdalena join me on stage. Together, we receive the award that makes our restaurant one of only two in Stavanger — and the only sushi restaurant in Norway — to achieve the much-coveted star.

"How will you celebrate the award?" asks a reporter.

"Dinner out with the new star winners," I answer. "There are many good restaurants here in Stockholm. When I get home, however," I hasten to add, "I'll celebrate the victory by eating simple, home-cooked Filipino food."

Director Michael Ellis said it well in his speech earlier that evening: "Fill your place with happy diners and Michelin star recognition follows." I can't think of a place more deserving of a star than home.

Sinigang sa Calamansi Sour and Savory Soup

Sinigang, from the word "sigang" meaning to cook in broth, is a hearty soup consisting of protein and vegetables. Chef Roger's sinigang reflects principles of minimalism: it is clear, light and delicate and is best enjoyed as the prelude to a meal.

TYPE OF DISH Sabaw (soup)
PREPARATION TIME 45 minutes +
  overnight or 6 hours soaking time
YIELD 6 servings

½ oz (15 g) kombu dried kelp
7 cups (1.68 L) water
8 oz (250 g) raw head-on shrimp,
  shelled, heads separated
2 oz (60 g) katsuobushi bonito flakes
3 tablespoons calamansi or lime juice
¼ teaspoon fish sauce
8 oz (250 g) salmon fillet, cut into 6
  pieces
¼ daikon radish, thinly sliced or 2
  globe radishes, sliced into 6 thin
  circles
3 okra pods, halved
6 leaves water spinach (kangkong), or
  spinach

1 Soak the kombu in the 7 cups of water. Place in the fridge and steep for 6 hours or overnight.
2 Strain the kombu water into a saucepan. Discard the kombu. Add the shrimp heads to the kombu water, cover, and boil over medium heat for 10 minutes. Remove from heat. Discard the shrimp heads.
3 Add the bonito flakes to the stock. Bring to a boil over medium-high heat, then remove from heat. Pour the stock through a strainer to remove the bonito flakes.
4 Return the stock to the pan and place over medium heat. Add the calamansi juice and fish sauce. Bring to a boil. Add more juice if you like a sourer taste.
5 Place the shrimp, salmon and radish in a strainer and simmer in the stock for about 3–5 minutes. Remove from the stock. Reduce heat to low and cover.
6 Blanch the okra and kangkong by dropping them in boiling water until tender but still vibrant green, 3 minutes for the okra and 40 seconds for the kangkong. Run the blanched vegetables under cold water.
7 Divide the vegetables, salmon and shrimp between soup bowls and pour in the hot stock. Serve immediately.

PER SERVING CALORIES 89KCAL | FATS 1.93G
SATURATED FAT 0.4G | PROTEIN 15.88G
CARBOHYDRATES 2.03G | FIBER 0.7G
SODIUM 247MG | SUGARS 0.62G
*sodium content computed also for discarded ingredients

Love, Loss and the Memories We Bake

Grace Guinto

Grace Guinto celebrates Filipino talent as co-founder of The Entree.Pinays, a collective of Aussie Filipinas working together to introduce Filipino culture to Australians; and Merkado, an online marketplace to showcase the work of Filipino creators. She is also the chief baking officer of Sweet Cora — a catering business specializing in desserts with a Filipino twist.

It's Christmas. I'm baking peppermint and choc chip cookies, calamansi meringue pies and gingerbread for a gingerbread house I'm making in the style of a traditional Filipino bahay kubo stilt house. The fragrance of cloves, the heady scent of cinnamon, the earthy smell of molasses and the delicious aroma of ginger fill the house. A shining star perched on top of the faux fir tree decked with jolly red poinsettias reaches for the ceiling. If only my circumstances were as merry and bright ...

This is my season of grief and longing — the time of year I lost my mama, Cora. Her passing seven years ago left a deep hole in my life. I still haven't come to terms with living in a world deprived of her infectious chuckles, her kind gaze, her warm embrace and, of course, her delectable cooking.

This year, the difficult period is exacerbated by more heartache for us all living in Victoria. Besides soaring December temperatures of over 104°F (40°C) intensified by droughts and catastrophic bushfires, we are also shackled by a global pandemic that has put our state into one of the harshest and longest lockdowns in the country and the world. Once pulsing with life, Melbourne, where I live, touted as the World's Most Liveable City, feels close to flatlining.

I stay at home and punctuate my days with baking. Mama's handwritten recipes become my lifeline, her love notes to me from the heavens above. Tracing my fingertip over her cursive writing,

> *"Mama's handwritten recipes become my lifeline, her love notes to me from the heavens above."*

"What I've missed most about my relationship with Mama has been resurrected through the love I now experience with my own daughter. I'm forever thankful for the sweet memories Mama has baked into my heart, mind and soul."

I close my eyes and imagine her once again in the kitchen, doling out a piece of her heart in every dish she cooks, infusing love into every morsel.

Cancer stole Mama away from us shortly after she was diagnosed. It wasn't fair. My mother wasn't supposed to be taken away from us so soon. She wasn't supposed to leave forever without meeting my only daughter, Stella Cora, whom I named after her. She and my daughter shouldn't have been robbed of one of life's greatest gifts — the bond between grandmother and granddaughter.

Little Stella Cora sneaks behind me in the kitchen as I'm putting the finishing touches to my gingerbread house. Thinking I can't see her, she pops a little of the sweet-and-spice-laden bread into her mouth. The mischievous grin on her face turns into a sheepish smile when she meets my eye and realizes she's been caught in the act. I scoop her up in my arms and shower her with kisses. She giggles. It strikes me that what I've missed most about my relationship with Mama has been resurrected through the love I now experience with my own daughter. I'm forever thankful for the sweet memories Mama has baked into my heart, mind and soul. Memories of her, my sweet Cora, help me get through a year of unprecedented distress.

Flipping through the pages of a notebook Mama took with her when she went to her chemo sessions, a sentence in her handwriting — the same cursive style as her recipe cards — leaps off the page. Amid the exhausting and debilitating treatment she had to endure, she wrote a quote that inspired hope. It read: "Life isn't fair but it's still good."

Mama was right. As I write, Melbourne records thirty consecutive days of zero new coronavirus cases, zero deaths and zero active cases. The city reawakens from its slumber and excitedly readies itself for a Covid-free Christmas.

Food for the Gods
No-Bake Date and Walnut Balls

Food for the Gods is traditionally a very rich dessert bar filled with dates and walnuts, usually enjoyed during Pasko (Christmas) season. But as Grace lives in Australia, where Christmas is in summer, she has lightened this holiday treat using oats instead of flour. Dates and walnuts are still the base, but peanut butter and honey, in lieu of butter and brown sugar, taste divine as binding and sweetening agents.

TYPE OF DISH Merienda (snack)
PREPARATION TIME 20 minutes
YIELD 12 energy balls

1 cup (225 g) pitted dates
⅔ cup (160 g) natural peanut butter
   (see tip, below)
⅓ cup (30 g) oats, rolled or
   quick-cooking
1 teaspoon vanilla extract
1 tablespoon chia seeds
2 teaspoons honey
¼ cup (30 g) walnuts
1 tablespoon pumpkin seeds, toasted
1 tablespoon shredded coconut

The era of American occupation saw a trend for cookbooks of American recipes using Filipino ingredients penned by expat American women and printed in the Philippines. In one of these books, *Good Cooking and Health in the Tropics* (1922), edited by Elsie Gaches, was a recipe for Food for the Gods. This is Grace Guinto's version.

PER SERVING CALORIES 161KCAL
FATS 9.56G | SATURATED
FAT 0.4G | PROTEIN 4.78G
CARBOHYDRATES 16.84G
FIBER 2.5G | SODIUM 62MG
SUGARS 10.36G

1 Soak the pitted dates in warm water for about 10 minutes, then drain.
2 Using a food processor, first chop the dates into small pieces. Add the peanut butter, oats, vanilla extract and chia seeds. Mix in the food processor with a drizzle of honey. If it looks too sticky to form into balls, add 1–2 more tablespoons of oats. If it looks too dry, add 1–2 more tablespoons of peanut butter or a drizzle of honey.
3 Once the mixture is the desired consistency, add the walnuts, pulsing quickly.
4 Roll into small balls and then sprinkle with the toasted pumpkin seeds and shredded coconut. You'll get approximately twelve Food for the Gods date-and-walnut balls, depending on the size and how much of the mixture you eat before rolling!

TIP
The peanut butter can be replaced with almond butter or other nut butters. Choose a natural peanut butter with no added sugar for a less sweet energy bite. Trust me, the dates add plenty of sweetness.

Fresh Lumpia
Shrimp and Veggie Rolls with Date and Peanut Sauce
by Jacqueline Chio-Lauri

Fresh lumpia is not fried and gets its crunch from fresh vegetables in season. This recipe calls for vegetables that are likely to be available anywhere you live. Feel free to change up the filling depending on what you can find in the market near you. If you want a vegan version, use tofu instead of shrimp and serve hubad (naked), without the wrapper.

TYPE OF DISH Merienda (snack)
PREPARATION TIME 1 hour
YIELD 12 servings

LUMPIA BATTER
1 cup (120 g) flour
Pinch of salt
2 eggs, beaten
1½ cups (360 ml) water
1½ tablespoons sunflower oil
 + a little extra to grease the pan

LUMPIA FILLING
2 tablespoons sunflower oil
3 cloves garlic, minced
1 onion, cut into slivers
8 oz (250 g) shrimp, shelled,
 deveined and chopped
8 oz (250 g) green beans,
 sliced thinly on the bias
1 carrot, cut into thin strips
4 oz (120 g) daikon radish or jicama,
 cut into strips
8 oz (250 g) bean sprouts
3 tablespoons coconut aminos
Pinch of salt
Pepper, to taste
12 romaine lettuce leaves
½ cup (75 g) peanuts, crushed

LUMPIA SAUCE
18 pitted dates
2½ cups (600 ml) warm water
5 cloves garlic, minced
3 tablespoons coconut aminos
2 tablespoons vegan peanut butter
Pinch of pepper
1 tablespoon vinegar

Make the batter

Mix the flour and salt in a mixing bowl with a whisk. Make a well in the middle and pour in the eggs. Add the 1½ cups of water and the 1½ tablespoons of oil and whisk with the eggs. Gradually mix in the flour until completely incorporated. Pour the batter mixture through a strainer into another bowl to remove lumps. Place in the refrigerator while preparing the lumpia filling.

Make the filling

Heat a large wok or skillet over medium heat. Add the oil. When the oil shimmers, add the garlic and onion and stir. When the onion turns translucent, add the shrimp. Stir-fry until the shrimp have turned opaque. Transfer the garlic, onion and shrimp to a plate with a slotted spoon and set aside. Leave oil in the wok. Turn the heat up to high. Add the green beans and carrot and stir-fry until the beans turn a vibrant green, about 2 minutes. Stir in the radish and bean sprouts. Add the coconut aminos, salt and pepper and stir until well blended, about 2 minutes. Mix the garlic, onion and shrimp back in. Remove from the heat. Do not cover.

Make the wrapper

Lightly grease an 8-inch (20 cm) nonstick pan. Place over medium-high heat. Whisk the batter to make sure of an even consistency. Pour enough batter to make a thin coating on the bottom of the pan (about ¼ cup [60 ml]). Lift, tilt and swirl the pan to spread the batter evenly and coat the bottom of the pan completely. Cook until the batter sets and the edges start to lift from the pan, around 1 minute. The lumpia wrapper should slip when

you shake the pan vigorously. Flip with the help of a turner or slip onto a plate and return to the pan with the uncooked side down. Cook for about 30 seconds then slide onto a plate. (Don't lose heart if the first one doesn't turn out well. The first crepe is often the worst.) Repeat until all the batter is finished. Stack the wrappers on top of each other.

Make the sauce

Puree the dates with the 2½ cups (600 ml) warm water in a blender. Transfer to a saucepan and boil over medium-high heat uncovered. Lower the heat to medium and add the garlic and coconut aminos. Simmer covered for 5 minutes. Stir in the peanut butter. Cook for another 2 minutes. If the sauce gets too thick, add a little water. Finish by stirring in pepper and vinegar.

Roll the lumpia

Set a wrapper on a plate. Lay a lettuce leaf on the upper middle part with a quarter of the leaf outside of the crepe. Place 2 tablespoons of filling on the lettuce along its rib. Fold the bottom end of the wrapper then fold over one side and roll tightly to the opposite side. Serve with the sauce, topped with crushed peanuts.

PER SERVING CALORIES 231KCAL
FATS 10.6G | SATURATED FAT 1.4G | PROTEIN 10.3G
CARBOHYDRATES 25.7G | FIBER 3.1G
SODIUM 236MG | SUGARS 10.8G

CHAPTER 4
Ensalada
Salads

Lettuce leaves drizzled with a mixture of oil and acid are a foreign concept in the tropical climes of the Philippines. But nutrient-rich green veggies, either raw or cooked, have always been part of the Filipino diet. The ones I came across growing up in Angeles City on the central plains of Luzon included dahon ng mustasa (mustard leaves), served fresh without dressing as sides for fried or grilled fish, accompanied with either a seasoned vinegar sawsawan (dipping sauce) or balo-balo, a condiment made of fermented rice and shrimp. Other fresh greens tossed raw into salads include young fronds of fiddlehead ferns called pako, strings of sea grape clusters called lato, sweet potato tops called talbos ng kamote, and the young yellow-green shoots of the mango tree called putat (my lola used to pick this nutritious tender foliage from the mango tree in our garden to eat mixed with her mango salad). Kangkong (water spinach or morning glory) — usually blanched, steamed or boiled — is also a common ingredient in Filipino ensaladas. If these varieties aren't available at your local market, some easier-to-find options recommended in this chapter will let you enjoy the wealth of health and delicious flavors of Filipino side salads.

Recipes in this chapter are closely in line with the 2019 American Heart Health program, which recommends that salads and side dishes should contain no more than 240 mg of sodium, 250 calories and 2 teaspoons of added sugars per serving.

An All-Inclusive Meal

Ria Dolly Barbosa

After notable stints in Las Vegas restaurants including Michael Mina, and Daniel Boulud Brasserie, and in Los Angeles at Sqirl and PCP, Ria Dolly Barbosa is opening her own Filipino restaurant, Peso Neighborhood and Lumpia Bar, in Honolulu, Hawaii where she is Executive Chef and VP.

> *"I suppose vegan food and I got off on the wrong foot. I became aware of it during a time when it masqueraded as burgers, hot dogs and the like."*

My sister Eza became vegan about six years ago. An omnivore myself, I scoffed at the notion initially. As a professional chef, I take pride in the ability to use any and all ingredients, coaxing out flavors from subtle to assertive depending on the dish and on my inspiration. When Eza made the decision to become vegan, it made family gatherings and eating together difficult, to say the least. I've worked in restaurants in the past where such dietary choices tended to be looked down on. In a lot of restaurants, the automatic way of dealing with vegans is to concoct some sort of sad vegetable pasta thrown together forlornly in a way that would make Oliver Twist's gruel look like a gourmet meal.

I remember a family trip to Redondo Beach. We feasted on Dungeness crab, shrimp, oyster, sea urchin, fish and steamed rice. We savored every oyster doused with freshly squeezed lemon juice, slurped the shrimp heads, and devoured the pockets of sweet crab coated with their mustard. Our family has always loved these seafood feasts eaten with our hands — to this day, they are some of my favorite family memories. But now Eza was a vegan. I looked over at my sister tucking into the plate of hummus, falafel, salad and pita she had picked up at a restaurant in our neighborhood on our way to Redondo. She was enjoying her meal as much as we were enjoying ours but even though we were all eating together, I couldn't help but feel a bit sad and disconnected from her.

> "[...] while I may not go vegan completely,
> I am becoming more aware of what
> I consume and what my future restaurant
> guests are consuming too."

I suppose vegan food and I got off on the wrong foot. I became aware of it during a time when it masqueraded as burgers, hot dogs and the like. They were vegetable versions of classics we all know and love, but often they were not delicious. I became curious. Where was all the good vegan food?

Those moments put me on a trajectory I hadn't anticipated. I knew I was not the first person to ask the question, "Is there vegan food that doesn't 'taste vegan'?" It became a bit of an obsession at first, but I decided to embark on a quest to try and create vegan dishes that tasted good, so that a loved one on a plant-based diet could sit down and share a thoughtfully created and delicious meal alongside their omnivorous dining companions that wasn't slop. That's when my sister became my muse.

Eza had made the switch for health and ethical reasons, which I can get behind. Our grandmother, Lola Ying, and uncle, Tito Tony (both on my mom's side), had passed away due to health problems within a short time of each other. That was when Eza decided to make changes to her diet. I have been thinking about it a lot lately as well and while I may not go vegan completely, I am becoming more aware of what I consume and what my future restaurant guests are consuming too. Thus, thoughtful, seasonal, Filipino-influenced food came to be in my repertoire. While not everything is vegan, it is food that is prepared with care and intended to be inclusive. Food that everyone in my family can happily enjoy together.

Warm Pinakbet Salad
Roasted Vegetable Salad with Bagoong-Calamansi Citronette

A fresher, lighter and brighter take on a classic favorite, this warm salad takes all the familiar pinakbet flavors, using a variety of textures and methods. This recipe has quite a lot of steps and components but fear not! It is absolutely worth it.

PREPARATION TIME 1 hour
YIELD 8 side salad servings
  or 4 main course servings

½ firm kabocha squash, about 3 lb
  (1.4 kg) peeled, seeded and 1-inch
  (2.5 cm) diced
5 tablespoons olive oil, divided
4 firm Asian eggplants, about 1 lb
  (500 g), sliced into ½-inch (1-cm)
  thick rounds
8 oz (250 g) long beans, cut into
  2-inch (5-cm) lengths
½ teaspoon sea salt, divided
5 tablespoons water
8–10 okra pods, trimmed and
  blanched
1 cup (75 g) halved cherry tomatoes
4 oz (120 g) mizuna or salad greens
4 oz (120 g) store-bought puffed
  rice cereal, plain, unsweetened, for
  garnish, optional

BAGOONG-CALAMANSI
CITRONETTE
4 teaspoons bagoong guisado shrimp
  paste
4 teaspoons calamansi juice
  or lime juice
⅓ cup (80 ml) olive oil

PER SERVING CALORIES 256KCAL
FATS 17.92G | SATURATED FAT 2.7G
PROTEIN 3.91G
CARBOHYDRATES 23.09G | FIBER 4.7G
SODIUM 246MG | SUGARS 5.69G

1 Preheat the oven to 350°F (175°C).
2 Toss the squash with about 1½ tablespoons of the olive oil in a large bowl and place on a baking sheet lined with a silicone baking mat or parchment paper.
3 Toss the eggplant and beans in the same bowl with another 1½ tablespoons of the olive oil and season with half of the sea salt.
4 Bake the squash for about 20–30 minutes, until soft enough to mash. Remove from the oven and puree in a food processor, adding the remaining 2 tablespoons of olive oil and the 5 tablespoons of water until smooth. Season lightly with the remaining sea salt to taste and set aside.
5 Turn the oven temperature to 400°F (200°C).
6 Place the eggplant and beans on the same baking sheet lined with a silicone baking mat or parchment paper. Bake in the oven for about 15–18 minutes until they both get a little color and are fork tender but not overcooked.
7 While the vegetables bake, make the citronette: Whisk the bagoong and calamansi or lime juice together, then whisk in the oil until well-blended. Set aside.
8 Remove the eggplant and beans from the oven and allow to cool slightly.
9 Spread the squash puree in a thick layer over the bottom of a serving platter.
10 Toss the baked eggplant, long beans, blanched okra, fresh tomatoes and mizuna together in a large enough bowl. Spread on top of the squash puree.
11 Drizzle with the citronette and garnish with a sprinkling of puffed rice, if using.

Pinakbet or pakbet, taken from an Ilocano word for "shriveled," is an indigenous vegetable stew from the Ilocos Region. Traditionally, freshly harvested backyard vegetables, such as eggplant, okra, bitter melon and winged beans, were steamed (no oil or frying involved!) and seasoned with fermented anchovies or shrimp, sparking an exciting interplay of flavors from the soil and the sea. The stew is typically served as a main dish, often replete with added protein, such as prawn or pork. The dish eventually became known throughout the nation and is now perhaps the most frequently appearing vegetable dish on the Filipino dining table. This recipe takes the pinakbet concept and reinterprets it as a salad.

Love at First Sight

Helen Orimaco-Pumatong

Helen Orimaco-Pumatong moved from Bohol in the Philippines to Vancouver, Canada when she was just six years old. She has worked as a chef instructor in the Hospitality Management Department at Vancouver Community College since 2010.

> *"I was sorry to miss my sister's big day, but I packed my bags. I knew that with Lola gone, it would be my last trip to the Philippines."*

All RSVPs were in. The final head count was set and the seating arrangement had been fixed. In a few days, my little sister would be walking down the aisle on the top deck of a yacht and I, her maid of honor, would do everything I could to make sure her big day was everything she had dreamed of. And of course I did, but not in the way I expected.

A few days before the wedding the phone rang bearing news that would change my life forever. It was a call from Bohol in the Philippines, my dad's hometown. Sadly, our grandmother had passed away, leaving us in a dilemma. Shouldn't at least one member of our family attend the funeral to pay our final respects to Lola? But with my sister's upcoming nuptials, who could go? I, as the eldest grandchild, thought it was my duty to represent our clan. I was sorry to miss my sister's big day, but I packed my bags. I knew that with Lola gone, it would be my last trip to the Philippines.

I'd just returned from a visit to the Philippines a week before to celebrate Lola's eighty-ninth birthday. It was a big event attended by relatives from different parts of the world. My aunt outdid herself and put out a spread that made me, a chef, gasp with delight — lechon suckling pig, a vast assortment of seafood and my favorite pancit noodle dishes.

When I arrived back on the island of Bohol, the wake for Lola was underway at a funeral home. A steady stream of people came in and out of the parlor throughout the day and night, many of

> "Life is full of these heartwarming moments [...] a look, a touch, a smile: fleeting like most things in life. Like love at first sight. You have to be present to feel it."

whom I'd never met before. At night time, some relatives kept vigil and organized activities such as mahjong and card games. I was sitting with them when a somewhat familiar guy with film-star good looks walked in with a friend.

I'd seen him before. A few weeks earlier when I'd been in Bohol for Lola's birthday, my cousin and I went for a ride around town on her scooter. Roaming Bohol with the gentle breeze caressing my face gave me a deeper appreciation for this beautiful island, fringed by clear turquoise-blue waters and powdery white sand beaches. Its seas, some of the most biodiverse on the planet, were filled with a mesmerizing variety of the freshest seafood. As the wheels of the motorbike crunched down a dirt road, I caught the unmistakable whiff of prawns cooking at a roadside turo-turo (eatery). I was saying something to my cousin when I halted mid-sentence. Walking out of the turo-turo was a dashing man — the perfect embodiment of the words "tall, dark and handsome."

"Who's that guy?" I asked my cousin.

"Oh, that's Toplak," she answered. She went on to profile the man offhandedly, not forgetting to drop a very interesting fact — "He's still single, you know." We giggled.

I had flown off to Vancouver the following day and thought no more about Toplak until he reappeared at the wake. I had no idea that my cousin, remembering how Toplak had caught my eye, had decided to play cupid and conspired to bring us together at the vigil. Toplak and I spent every moment after the funeral together until it was time for me to go home.

At the airport to catch my return flight to Vancouver, the flight was overbooked and passengers who gave up their seats were offered an extra free round-trip ticket as compensation if they rebooked on a different flight. I didn't think twice. I snapped up the opportunity and dashed back to the island, happy to spend a few more days with Toplak.

A year and a half later, we walked down the aisle. I gazed into Toplak's almond-shaped brown eyes and he gazed back into mine as we said, "I do." The expression on his face made my heart skip a beat. It is the same expression I will behold many times more in our life together — I'll see it when he looks at our newborn as he cradles him in his arms for the first time and again when he meets and holds our second-born. Life is full of these heartwarming moments. Most, I should add, don't come as big events like weddings and funerals; they pop up more subtly — a look, a touch, a smile: fleeting, like most things in life. Like love at first sight. You have to be present to feel it.

Ensaladang Mangga at Hipon
Poached Prawns with Mango-Fennel Salad

Mangoes are not only eaten as fruits in the Philippines, but also as vegetables. Mangoes used in ensaladang mangga (mango salad) are usually firm and crisp and not quite ripe, with more Vitamin C and antioxidants than ripe ones, making them heart-healthier. Here Helen amps up the flavors of this salad by simmering the prawns in acid, aromatics and spice.

PREPARATION TIME 50 minutes
YIELD 6 side dish servings

POACHED PRAWNS
1 bulb fennel, roughly chopped
1 large yellow onion, diced large
1 carrot, diced large
2 celery stalks, diced large
1 lemon, halved
4 calamansi, halved; or 2 limes, quartered
¼ cup (60 ml) rice vinegar
3 bay leaves
1 tablespoon whole black peppercorns
1 tablespoon salt
1½ gallons (6 L) cold water
1 lb (500 g) 21/25 count raw prawns, shelled and deveined

MANGO-FENNEL SALAD
1 large firm mango, cut into thin strips
3 roma tomatoes, cored and thinly sliced
1 small red onion, thinly sliced
1 fennel bulb, shaved thinly on a mandolin
1 bunch red radish, shaved thinly on a mandolin, divided
1 bunch cilantro, for garnish

PER SERVING INCLUDING PRAWNS
BUT NOT POACHING INGREDIENTS
CALORIES 270KCAL | FATS 18.6G
SATURATED FAT 1.9G | PROTEIN 9G
CARBOHYDRATES 19.77G FIBER 2.6G
SODIUM 100MG | SUGARS 16G

CALAMANSI-HONEY DRESSING
¼ cup (85 g) honey
Juice of 4 calamansi or 1 lime (about 3 tablespoons)
1 small shallot, finely chopped
Salt and ground pepper to taste
1 red Thai chili, finely chopped, optional
½ cup (120 ml) grapeseed oil

Make the poached prawns

1 Place all the ingredients, except the prawns, in a large stock pot. Bring to a boil over high heat then turn down the heat to the lowest setting and let simmer.
2 Place half the prawns in a strainer and submerge them gently into the simmering stock. Cook for about 2–3 minutes, until the prawns turn pink and opaque. Remove and shake off the excess liquid. Place on a plate to cool. Repeat with the other half of the prawns. Once cooled, place in a lidded container and put in the fridge.

Make the salad

Place all the salad ingredients, except the cilantro and a little of the radish, in a large bowl. Mix.

Make the dressing

1 Place all the ingredients except the oil in a mason jar. Close the jar tight and shake to mix. Add the oil. Close the jar tight and shake again to mix thoroughly.
2 Pour half of the dressing over the salad and toss lightly. Divide onto 6 plates. Toss the rest of the dressing with the prawns. Arrange the prawns on top of the salad.
3 Garnish with the shaved radish and cilantro.

OPTION
You can simply pan-steam the prawns, halabos style. Place ¼ cup (60 ml) water with a pinch of salt in a large skillet or wok over high heat. Bring the water to a rapid boil. Add the prawns and cover. Turn off the heat. Allow to steam until the prawns turn pink and opaque, about 2 minutes. Drain.

The Good Mother

Mae Magnaye Williams

Mae Magnaye Williams is the chef and creator of the popular cooking website foodwithmae.com. In 2016, she appeared on national television in the UK with British cooking-show host Mary Berry, teaching her how to make the Filipino lechon roasted pig. She is a founding member of the Filipino Food Movement in the UK.

"My mother and for a shorter period, also my father, left the country when I was seven years old to take care of other people's children while one auntie took care of me."

"Why aren't you happy to see me when I come home?" was the question my husband Adrian asked me when he returned home from work that day. Or perhaps he'd said, "Why are you always angry when I come home?"

I didn't answer. Not because I didn't know the answer to his question, but because I had no energy to reply. Motherhood was taking its toll on me. Layer upon layer of dark, pent-up feelings of doubt, resentment, despair and overwhelming fatigue were building up inside me. That day, like most other days, I felt I was about to explode. Sometimes I did. But that day I didn't, simply because I had no energy.

Throughout that day, my one-year-old baby was unable to settle because she was teething. No amount of teething gel or cold carrots was helping. As if that wasn't enough, her three-year-old sister wouldn't stop bombarding me with questions, clinging on to me like a baby koala! While my youngest tested my patience, my oldest tested my hearing! I'm proud of my older daughter's advanced verbal skills, but that day I could have done with a little silence.

I had no one to turn to. My mother lived in Kent, two hours away from our home in London and none of my friends were mothers. When Adrian got back from work, I was out of juice and all I wanted to do was cry.

I had made a conscious decision to be a stay-at-home mom, mainly because I had grown up away from my mother and I didn't want that for my daughters. I wanted to be there for them all the

> **"Once a month, after I tucked the girls in bed and kissed them goodnight (luckily, they were good sleepers!), I hosted supper clubs in my home, sharing the dishes of my childhood in the Philippines with my guests in the UK."**

time, for all the special occasions — for birthdays, graduations, first menstruation — all the events when I had wished that my mother could have been there for me.

The story of my childhood is not unique in the Philippines. Due to the shortage of jobs that pay a decent living wage in the country, a lot of parents leave their kids with relatives and take jobs overseas. That's what had happened to my sister and me. My mother and, for a shorter period, also my father, left the country when I was seven years old to look after other people's children while one auntie took care of me and another auntie took care of my little sister.

Four years later, when the Danish family my parents worked for in Taiwan moved to the UK, my father's services were no longer needed and so he returned home to the Philippines, while my mother stayed on with them to continue looking after their children. During the years that followed, it was my father who took the role of both mother and father to me. He taught me how to clean the house, wash clothes and, most importantly, he taught me how to cook. Sadly, he passed away when my kids were little. I broke into pieces.

Although I sought professional help to get me through my grief and those difficult years when my children were very young, it was cooking that eventually helped me get back on an even keel. When the girls were older, I'd drop them off at school and then I'd spend the day doing things I loved, such as making food. When it was time

to pick up my little ones from school, I was able to be the best possible mother for the rest of the day. Once a month, after I tucked the girls in bed and kissed them goodnight (luckily, they were good sleepers!), I hosted supper clubs in my home, sharing the dishes of my childhood in the Philippines with my guests in the UK.

Now that my daughters are at about the same age as I was when I was motherless, a harsh inner voice often creeps into my head questioning my worth as a mother. Is this the right way to do it? Am I bringing my girls up right? Am I too strict or am I too soft? To be honest, I don't know. All I know is there's no perfect mother. We just try to do the best we can in the circumstances we are given. Having two daughters, just like my mother, has given me a newfound respect for her. Moving away from her children must have been the most excruciating experience in the world. Yet, she did it in the hopes of providing us with a better life and ultimately, she did. "Maraming salamat, Mama" — thank you so much!

Ensaladang Puso ng Saging
Banana Blossom Salad with Coconut Dressing

Banana blossom, or banana heart, is touted as "the next star of the vegan meat world" due to its fishlike flakiness and mouthfeel. In traditional Philippine cooking, the blossom is not used as a meat substitute but as a vegetable. It is typically added to meat dishes, such as kare-kare and sinigang, giving them a veggie boost. This ensalada takes elements from various Philippine banana-blossom cooking preparations — such as kinilaw (marinating with acid) and ginataan (cooking with coconut milk) — resulting in a salad that is uniquely Mae's.

PER SERVING CALORIES 61.67KCAL
FATS 3.37G | **SATURATED FAT** 2.2G
PROTEIN 1.47G
CARBOHYDRATES 5.72G | **FIBER** 2.4G
SODIUM 234MG | **SUGARS** 0.88G

PREPARATION TIME 20 minutes
YIELD 6 servings

2 cans banana blossom in brine, about 18 oz (550 g) drained weight, rinsed thoroughly and drained
1 teaspoon safflower oil
4/5 cup (200ml) light coconut milk
Juice of 1 lemon
1 small red onion, minced
1 clove garlic, minced
Pinch of salt
Pinch of ground pepper
1 tablespoon fresh chives, chopped

1 Pat the banana blossoms with kitchen paper towels to dry.
2 Brush a griddle pan with the safflower oil. Heat the pan on the stove over high heat.
3 Grill the banana blossom until charred on all sides.
4 In a bowl, make the coconut dressing by mixing the coconut milk, lemon juice, onion, garlic, salt and pepper. Whisk until well blended.
5 Thinly slice the banana blossoms crosswise. Toss with the coconut dressing.
6 Sprinkle the chives over the salad.

For the Bitter (Melon) Moments in Life

Cynthia Cherish Malaran

Cynthia Cherish Malaran aka DJ CherishTheLuv is a radio host and DJ for Heritage Radio Network, the world's pioneer food radio station. Her shows, *Wedding Cake* and *Primary Food*, center on conversations about food, as well as activities that nourish our heart, mind and soul.

There is a short list of foods I could not stand as a Filipino-American kid who was conceived, born and raised in New York City. I would throw a legit tantrum if you tried to feed me something that wasn't American; watery rice, ginger, onions, celery, okra, bagoong guisado shrimp paste, vinegar, anything to do with fish, and most of all . . . ampalaya bitter melon. If my mom, Adel, made adobo, somehow it made us kids want pizza or McDonalds even more. And when the dinuguan pork blood stew was uncovered at a party, all of us kids ran screaming.

Now, as an adult, with evolved, grown-person taste buds, I crave these foods. My DNA has taken over. My emotional eating is related to my aging parents and my need to reconnect to my culture in order to heal. OK, I still struggle with celery, but maybe because that's not a typical veggie my grandparents from Bohol grew up eating. And I think this is important — eating what we're biologically familiar with. Family meals prepared by elders speak to us in a way that keeps us holistically healthy.

When my mother had a stroke in 2001, I broke my vegetarian diet the second she was well enough again to cook the chicken adobo we grew up with. It never tasted so good. The thought of losing her and missing the things she cooked, the way she cooked it (because all the adobos are different!) was heartbreaking. But here we are,

"My emotional eating is related to my aging parents and my need to reconnect to my culture in order to heal."

> "Eating Mom's food feels like a reset inside me; it's true comfort food, especially when the flavors somehow connect to what I'm going through."

more than twenty years later (saying "wow!' as I type this) and we are still being blessed by that adobo made by Mom.

Like Mom, my life has had its ups and downs and I found my healing through food. Eating Mom's food feels like a reset inside me; it's true comfort food, especially when the flavors somehow connect to what I am going through. I find that when going through hard times, tired times and stressed-out times, I turn away from sweet things. I crave VINEGAR! Vinegar is sharp, alert, strong, brave, energizing. Everything I need when feeling burdened.

Unfortunately, at these times, I also crave fat, fried foods and salt. So why not balance it with one of my favorite uses of vinegar — ampalaya bitter melon salad! Yes! One of my most hated food from childhood. Oh, how I love it now when my mom makes it! The acidity of the vinegar cuts through any heaviness I am feeling and it makes the rice come to life. When Mom makes it, it's truly a hands-on experience, with the massaging of salt to lessen the bitterness — a sweet metaphor for Mom taking the sadness and bitterness out of my day, so I can stand strong. I find that when I go to parties where Filipino food is served, having a sour and savory atchara relish or ampalaya bitter melon salad helps me curb my appetite, eat more veggies, eat less lechon roast pig and less dessert, hence less sodium, cholesterol, sugar, heartburn and guilt. Vinegary salads save the day.

Ampalaya Pickled Bitter Melon Salad

This is how Cynthia's mom, Adel, makes her favorite ampalaya salad.

PREPARATION TIME
  20 minutes + 1 hour marinating time
YIELD 6 side-dish servings

2 bitter melons, approximately
  8 inches (20 cm) long
2 tablespoons sea salt
½ cup (120 ml) white vinegar
2 tablespoons white sugar
Pinch of adobo seasoning, optional
½ piece fresh ginger, peeled and
  cut into thin strips
1 firm tomato, thinly sliced
½ medium red onion, diced
½ carrot, julienned
½ red bell pepper, diced

Prepare the ampalaya

1 Cut the ends off the bitter melons and discard. Cut
  the bitter melons in half lengthwise. With a metal
  spoon, scoop out the seeds and white flesh. Slice
  the melons into crescents about 2–3 mm thick,
  depending on how crunchy you like each bite. Place
  the slices in a large bowl and sprinkle with the 2
  tablespoons of salt. Massage the salt into the bitter
  melon firmly and squeeze until the flesh is a deeper,
  translucent green and dark green juice builds up
  in the bowl. Pour out the juice and rinse the bitter
  melon in running water three times to wash away
  the salt and bitter juices that have been extracted.
  Put the bowl of bitter melon aside.

Prepare the salad

1 In a separate bowl, mix the vinegar, sugar and
  adobo seasoning if using, until the sugar has
  dissolved. Add the ginger, tomato, onion, carrot and
  red pepper and mix until well blended.
2 Pour the vinegared veggie mix over the bitter melon
  and toss to evenly coat. Add vinegar to taste, if
  needed. Set aside to marinate in the refrigerator
  for at least an hour, or until ready to serve. Serve
  alongside your protein dishes and rice.

PER SERVING, NOT INCLUDING SALT
USED TO PREPARE THE BITTER MELON
CALORIES 37KCAL | FATS 0.18G
SATURATED FAT 0G | PROTEIN 0.86G
CARBOHYDRATES 7.8G | FIBER 1.6G
SODIUM 157MG | SUGARS 5.16G

Atchara Beetroot Relish

by Jacqueline Chio-Lauri

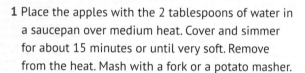

Any plate of protein cooked with dry heat looks forlorn without a mound of atchara beside it. Atchara generally refers to fruits or vegetables preserved without refrigeration. It is also the name of a specific relish made of grated green papaya, the most popular atchara. The pickle, though originating from the Indian achar, may have been introduced to the Philippines by early Indonesian settlers. This recipe uses beetroot — naturally sweet and a great source of nutrients — as it's often easier to find than green papaya. Atchara made with beetroot has the spiced sweet and sour taste we love about papaya atchara without the added sugar.

PREPARATION TIME 1 hour
YIELD 6 servings or 1½ cups

2 Pink Lady or other sweet apples, peeled, cored and chopped
2 tablespoons water
1 large beetroot, about 8 oz (250 g), steamed, peeled and cut into thin strips
1 small carrot, cut into strips
2-inch (5-cm) piece ginger, peeled and grated
1 clove garlic, minced
¼ cup (60 ml) coconut or cane vinegar
½ teaspoon salt
½ teaspoon freshly ground pepper

1 Place the apples with the 2 tablespoons of water in a saucepan over medium heat. Cover and simmer for about 15 minutes or until very soft. Remove from the heat. Mash with a fork or a potato masher.

2 Add the remaining ingredients to the saucepan and place over medium heat. Mix, cover and allow to simmer for 15 minutes, stirring occasionally. Turn off the heat and let cool. Serve immediately or store in a sterilized jar with a lid in the fridge. It will keep for two weeks.

PER SERVING CALORIES 48KCAL
FATS 0.17G | SATURATED FAT 0G
PROTEIN 0.67G | CHOLESTEROL 0MG
CARBOHYDRATES 11.57G | FIBER 2.3G
SODIUM 217MG | SUGARS 8.24G

CHAPTER 5

Gulay

Vegan and Semi-Vegetarian Meals

In the Philippines, you'll find delicious regional vegetable stews bursting with color and texture and using all parts of the plant from root to fruit. But these vegetable dishes are rarely vegetarian. The Filipino way of cooking vegetables often starts with guisa or sautéing garlic, onion, pork and/or shrimp. Most, if not all vegetable stews also rely on fish or seafood derivatives such as patis or bagoong guisado shrimp paste, for flavor. However, the good news for vegans is that Filipino food is not dairy dependent, and recipes can be made vegan-friendly by simply leaving out or replacing the meat or fish elements.

The 2020–2025 Dietary Guidelines for Americans recommend plant-based eating patterns. Plant-based diets have been proven to prevent and reverse heart disease, improve cholesterol and lower blood pressure. All contributors in this chapter rose to the challenge of not only using mainly plant-based ingredients, but also reducing salt without sacrificing savor.

Recipes in this chapter are closely in line with the 2019 American Heart Health program, which recommends that a main dish should contain no more than 600 mg of sodium, 500 calories, and 2 teaspoons of added sugars per serving.

Home Is Where It Is

Benedicto Mariñas

Benedicto Mariñas is a classically trained Cordon Bleu chef with a university diploma in gastronomy from the University of Reims in France. He travels around the world for his current book project about his search for the perfect meal, and is the author of the cookbook *The Malian Kitchen*.

> *"The Moringa tree represented everything of home I now missed. I yearned to be with my mother, whose embrace I would still give anything to feel one last time."*

"What has been your biggest accomplishment so far?" asked someone I'd just met at a dinner party. I was stumped. No stranger had ever asked me that before.

I thought my biggest accomplishment was having visited every country but three represented in the last Miss Universe beauty pageant. Maybe that's an odd metric, but it means I've been to ninety-one countries. I consider being so widely traveled a massive accomplishment because exploring the world was a childhood dream for me.

I was born and raised in the northern Philippines. My hometown was a quintessential farming region in our impoverished but beautiful nation. Our way of life was simple. Only one family in my village had a TV set. In this house, along with the entire neighborhood, I watched my first Miss Universe pageant and discovered snippets of the enthralling culture of every participating nation. The show ignited my vagabond spirit.

I've lived happily and productively outside my homeland for many years, made myself at home in many different cities. It wasn't until more than twenty years after leaving my native country that I first experienced the homesickness that, at least temporarily, afflicts most of my fellow expatriates. That was when I traveled to Mali to work as a culinary and nutrition specialist.

I arrived in Bamako, Mali a few minutes after two o'clock in the morning. Bara, the hosting organization's director, met me at the airport and brought me directly to the place that would

> **"This was the very dish my mother prepared every time I caught some ailment as a child. Even when we couldn't afford chicken and Mother had to make tinola without it, this dish still worked its magic."**

serve as my home base. When he left, I suddenly became giddy at the realization that I was in West Africa for the first time. Any semblance of sleepiness vanished. I went out and sat down in the small garden to wait for my first glimpse of the sun rising over Malian soil. It did not take long, and as the dawn slowly illuminated my surroundings, something caught my eye — a tree.

Like a mirage, its leaves, in various shades of green, danced to the gentle rhythm of the early-morning breeze. Its trunk stood proud and regal, its branches reassuring in their arcing architectural arrangement. And the scent! Its fragile sweetness made me feel weak. Suddenly, I was once again a preadolescent beauty-pageant fanatic in a bucolic corner of the world, sashaying on the rice fields, waving to an imaginary audience with one of this tree's blossoms tucked behind my left ear, preparing for my imagined future as Miss Universe.

There was no mistaking what I was looking at. A Moringa tree!

A longing to be back in the land I still call home overtook me. The ferocity of homesickness jolted me to my core, as though someone had punched me in the gut. I had to exert effort to breathe. The Moringa tree represented everything of home I now missed. I yearned to be with my mother, whose embrace I would still give anything to feel one last time. She had passed away a year after I left home, and at that point it had been impossible to go back to pay my last respects. Getting up to stand under the Moringa tree, I sobbed with abandon like the orphan that I was,

like I had when I heard of her death that sunny July day on Hong Kong's Lantau Island.

I heard movement from a hut nearby. This outbuilding was, I had learned earlier, the living space of Togo, the man who would be my housekeeper. "Do you want your breakfast now, sir?" he asked in practiced English.

As Togo was about to head for the kitchen, I pointed at the Moringa tree and, asked him to harvest the young leaves. He looked puzzled but granted my request.

I went in to prepare my first meal in Mali myself. The fridge was filled with essentials, including chicken, but not rice, so chicken tinola soup with Moringa leaves and fonio, a locally cultivated grain, was my first breakfast in Mali. This was the very dish my mother prepared every time I caught some ailment as a child. Even when we couldn't afford chicken and Mother had to make tinola without it, this dish still worked its magic.

I wanted to share it with Togo, who initially resisted my invitation to sit down with me at the table. A whiff of the Moringa-flavored soup, however, and his resolve vanished. We devoured the dish like two brothers long deprived of their favorite comfort food. And when Togo, sweating profusely, exclaimed, "A kadi!" — the first Bambara phrase I learned, meaning "delicious" — I knew I was home.

Vegan Dinuyduy Squash and Moringa Stew

Dinuyduy, also known as duyduy or dinuyduyan, is a popular stew in the Ilocos region of the Philippines. Squash is its main ingredient; pork, minced beef or fried fish the favorite sahog or flavoring agents; ampalaya (bitter melon) leaves or sometimes talbos ng camote (sweet potato tops) the default greens; and patis (fish sauce) the common seasoning. For this vegan version of the dish, Benedicto uses Moringa instead of ampalaya leaves, and vegan dashi stock, which is relatively lower in sodium than patis. You will need to make the stock in advance.

PREPARATION TIME 30 minutes + at
  least 6 hours to make the Vegan Dashi
  Stock
YIELD 4 servings

VEGAN DASHI STOCK
⅓ oz (10 g) dried kombu kelp, lightly
  brushed off with a paper towel
4 small dried shiitake mushrooms, lightly
  brushed off with a paper towel
4 cups (960 ml) water

STEW
1 teaspoon olive oil
2 cloves garlic, diced
1 red onion, diced
1 small tomato, diced
½ a kabocha squash, diced
3 cups (720 ml) Vegan Dashi Stock
  (recipe below)
2 cups (60 g) fresh Moringa leaves
  or spinach
Pinch of salt and pepper

PER SERVING CALORIES 350KCAL
FATS 1.4G | SATURATED FAT 0.2G
PROTEIN 2.2G | CARBOHYDRATES 9.4G
FIBER 2.3G | SODIUM 52MG | SUGARS 3.2G

For the vegan dashi stock

1 In a saucepan, soak the kombu and mushrooms in the water overnight or for at least 6 hours.
2 Boil over medium-high heat then turn off the heat. Allow to cool.
3 Take the mushrooms out of the liquid and chop them finely. Strain the liquid using a cheesecloth over a sieve and a bowl to make sure you have a clear broth. Mix the mushrooms with the strained liquid.

For the stew

1 Heat the olive oil in a large pan over medium-high heat until it shimmers. Add the garlic, onion and tomato and stir-fry until the onion starts to caramelize and the tomatoes soften. Add the squash and stir until well mixed.
2 Pour in the Vegan Dashi Stock with mushrooms. Cover the pan for a few minutes or until the squash is tender. Fish out a few pieces of the squash, place on a plate and mash with a fork. Add the mashed squash back in the pan to provide thickness to the broth.
3 Add salt and pepper to taste. Add Moringa leaves and stir. Turn off heat and serve.

Magic Sarap

Joel Javier

Chef Joel Javier and his wife Rachel Javier are the team behind the awe-inspiring, Brooklyn-based food business, Flip Eats — their story of new American-Filipino cuisine. They create unique dining experiences for guests with seasonally driven and global flavors, while paying homage to treasured Filipino fare.

"It continues to baffle me how much we use meat or seafood in practically all our dishes. And worse, how little we revere the great and mighty vegetable."

"What vegetarian dishes do you have?" I asked the waiter as I browsed through the menu at a small restaurant in Metro Manila.

"Here po Sir, in the vegetables section," he replies.

I look at where he's pointing. There's dinengdeng, a vegetable stew (oh, but it has fish); tortang talong, an eggplant omelet (but wait, it's with ground beef). How about munggo, mung beans? (Nope, it has shrimp). And then of course, there's the most famous "vegetarian" Filipino dish of all . . . pinakbet, which yup, you guessed it, has pork and shrimp.

This was a typical scene Rachel and I constantly encountered when we tried eating traditional food anywhere in the Philippines. It continues to baffle me how much we use meat or seafood in practically all our dishes. And worse, how little we revere the great and mighty vegetable.

Luckily, my mom, a big advocate of nutritious food, prepared family meals primarily centered around plant-based ingredients. When I was accepted into culinary school, Mom jumped at the opportunity to give me an "early start" by tasking me to cook our family dinners. But because she did the grocery shopping, vegetables of course, were the main ingredients. This laid the foundation of the food choices I made throughout my life.

After college, while under the rigorous French training of David Bouley, I learned some things that I still continue to live by: vegetable purees and olive oil create something rich and light; not all potatoes are created equally; and carrots

> ## "[...] now, as a Filipino-American, no matter what I cook, no matter how many vegetables I use, I'm confident that the dishes I make are truly Filipino."

cooked in carrot juice will really taste like carrots. Then came the biggest force to be reckoned with — my mentor, no other than the king of green markets himself — chef Bill Telepan. Bill not only deepened my love of vegetables; he deepened my appreciation for their qualities. I had never coaxed flavors out of veggies as well as I did when working with him. I learned to let the vegetables sing, let them lead and let them shine on their own merit, rather than merely tossing them into a dish to support proteins.

Finding my vision as a chef, however, led me to a crossroads. I was torn between the food I had learned to love since leaving home and my love of Filipino food. Though I had easy access to my American comfort foods, my cravings for dishes like adobo, kare-kare and sinigang never waned. So, I tried to cook them. I made "traditional" versions. I made Filipino-American versions. But whatever version I made, it was never quite right. The American side of me and my love of vegetables were too pronounced for comfort. Ultimately, a core essence to my dishes was missing. I ventured out to find it.

My wife Rachel and I traveled to the Philippines and spent two years exploring different regions of the motherland. We bunked in Rachel's family home and walked to the street corner at dusk to try whatever the young street vendor was hawking that night. Once a week, we took a jeepney to the palengke (market) to buy the freshest locally grown vegetables. We visited friends, sometimes just to check if their santol

tree had born any fruits. We toured sugar cane farms and morning wet markets and chatted with fishermen, heirloom yayas (maids passed down through generations who know all of the family recipes) and of course the lolas (grandmas) and lolos (grandpas). We dove deep into the everyday culture, eating everyday food.

When we returned to the US, I couldn't have been happier with the first dish I made. I had found it — the magic "sarap" or deliciousness that made my Filipino food taste like home. I wish there was a word to describe exactly what the magic is. Perhaps that word is the Philippines herself. When I immerse myself into who she is, she becomes a part of me. Her ways, her thoughts, her needs, her essence. And now, as a Filipino-American, no matter what I cook, no matter how many vegetables I use, I'm confident that the dishes I make are truly Filipino.

I no longer see my predominant use of vegetables in my dishes as contrary to Philippine cuisine. Instead, I see it as a connection — a bridge that binds Filipino flavors with high quality, local produce, creating healthy and flavorful dishes that might not look traditional, yet somehow, still remind me of home.

Eggplant Adobo Salad

Chef Joel didn't like eggplant as a kid. Later he realized it's a great meat alternative for adobo because it mimics the texture of pork fat with a richness and unctuousness that other vegetables don't have. Now the dish is a firm favorite!

PREPARATION TIME 30 minutes
YIELD 4 servings

ADOBO DRESSING
1½ tablespoons low sodium soy
 sauce or coconut aminos
3 tablespoons red wine vinegar or
 vinegar of choice
½ cup (120 ml) low-sodium vegetable
 stock (or 1 teaspoon Pinoy Powder, page
 15, mixed with ½ cup water)
1 tablespoon garlic powder
2 tablespoons extra virgin olive oil
2 fresh or 4 dry bay leaves
1 tablespoon toasted cracked black pepper
1½-inch (4-cm) piece ginger, peeled and
 minced
6 cloves garlic, crushed

EGGPLANT
4 Asian eggplants, about 1 lb (500 g) total,
 cut into ½-inch (1-cm) disks
1 tablespoon onion powder
1 tablespoon garlic powder
2 teaspoons brown or coconut sugar
1 tablespoon cracked black pepper
¼ cup (60 ml) oil with a high smoking
 point (sunflower, avocado or grapeseed)
10 cloves garlic, thinly sliced
2 fresh or 4 dry bay leaves

SALAD
½ bunch watercress
1½ cups (225 g) cherry tomatoes, halved
1 tablespoon toasted garlic (found in
 Asian groceries), optional

PER SERVING CALORIES 330KCAL
FATS 21.4G | SATURATED FAT 2.6G
PROTEIN 7.4G | CARBOHYDRATES 32.62G
FIBER 7.3G | SODIUM 270MG | SUGARS 13.4G

Make the adobo dressing

1 Mix all the ingredients in a pot and bring to a boil. Once the mixture boils, simmer for 15 minutes, strain and let cool. Whisk well before using.

Make the eggplant

1 Press the eggplant disks with paper towels to remove as much moisture as possible. Mix the onion powder, garlic powder, sugar and black pepper in a bowl. Season the eggplants with half of this seasoning mixture. Set aside the rest.

2 Start with a cold pan and add the oil and the garlic. Turn the heat up to medium. Cook for 1–2 minutes or until the garlic is golden. Transfer the garlic to a bowl. Turn the heat to medium high. Place the bay leaves and eggplant in the pan without overlapping; cook in batches if necessary. (Use a rubber spatula so as not to break up the eggplant.) Occasionally flip the eggplants over to prevent the sugar from burning too quickly. Once the eggplant is soft, cooked through and golden-brown, transfer to a bowl. Immediately add half of the adobo dressing while the eggplant is still hot. Lightly mix together. Set aside and let cool to room temperature.

To assemble

1 Place the watercress and tomatoes in a large bowl. Pour over the remaining vinaigrette and toss. Add the remaining half of the seasoning mixture. Place the eggplant on a serving plate. Add the watercress-tomato mix on top. Garnish with toasted garlic (optional).

2 Serve each portion with a side of Vegan Ube Pandesal (see page 42).

MeKeni! Mangan Tana!

Francis Sibal

Born and raised in Tarlac in the Philippines, Francis Zarate Sibal moved to Los Angeles when he was ten. He earned a Bachelor's Degree in Sociology at San Jose State University and was sous chef at Google Cloud in Sunnyvale California. Currently, he is Executive Chef at CZ Ranch in Tarlac.

"Ma makes cooking look like pleasure, not a chore. She carries out each step with precision and purpose."

"Frans, meKeni! Mangan ta na!" cried out my mom from across the hall. It's been years since we moved to California, but every morning for as long as I remember, she'd call me to come and eat in her native Kapampangan.

Her voice would jar me awake. But it was the whiff of roasted garlic and the breakfast it brought to mind that made me lift my legs off the bed and follow my nose to the kitchen.

On June 12, 2001, I found Ma stooped at the kitchen table. She was staring down at her hands with an expression on her face that alarmed me.

"Frans," she said. She looked at me with tears rolling down her face. My heart pounded.

"I have cancer," she continued.

Countless questions raced through my head while I stood staring at her.

When it struck me that my reaction might have been mistaken for callousness, I ran to her and wrapped my arms around her tightly. She was trembling. It wasn't like her to break down. Ma is the strongest person I know. Her inner strength comes from a power greater than herself — her faith. She always told us to leave things to God, and that's what I did.

My mom, Adelaida, is the reason I fell in love with food preparation. She has taught me the art of cooking from the heart since I was little.

"We don't just cook to feed the stomach," is what she always says. "We cook from the heart to feed the soul."

Ma makes cooking look like a pleasure, not a chore. She carries out each step with precision

> ## "My mom, Adelaida [always says], 'We don't just cook to feed the stomach. We cook from the heart to feed the soul'."

and purpose. She doesn't mind waiting longer, washing more pots and going the extra mile to make sure the food she puts on the table is the best it can possibly be. Her devotion to cooking never ebbed even during chemo. After long debilitating hours of treatment, she'd return home and cook.

Ma fought hard to defeat the disease. She endured chemo and a mastectomy and was cleared of cancer a year after her diagnosis.

Thirteen years later, in 2014, I packed my bags and headed for our hometown in Tarlac. I needed to reconnect with my roots. My family had uprooted itself from the Philippines in 1992, a year after the cataclysmic Mount Pinatubo eruption had buried tracts of land, claimed lives and destroyed the homes of more than a hundred thousand people. The Philippine government had refused to renew the lease of the Clark Air Base in Angeles City, then a US military facility that also suffered heavy damage from the volcanic ashfall. Everyone who worked at the base was to be repatriated to the US, and Filipino civilian workers like my mom were issued special US visas. My parents took it as a ticket to a better life for our family.

When I returned to the US after my trip to the Philippines, to my surprise, Ma was not at the door to greet me. Instead, she was in bed in her room. She'd had another mastectomy. The cancer had returned.

It's been a continuous struggle with cancer again since then. I live with constant anxiety that it might defeat Ma. After finding out she had tried to shield me from the news of the relapse, I couldn't shake off that eerie feeling every time I left her that each goodbye might be the last.

Cancer didn't only invade Ma's body; it has also metastasized within me in the form of fear. If I wanted to help Ma and really be there for her, letting fear stand in the way wasn't doing it. I needed to accept I could do nothing to control Ma's cancer, but I could do a lot to make every moment spent with her special. Many of those moments take place at the dining table.

Ma's battle against cancer ended five years later. In the summer of 2019, her doctor declared her fully recovered and cancer free, thanks to God! Together with my dad, she moved back to the Philippines, where she is enjoying a well-deserved retirement. Across the Pacific Ocean, I can almost hear Ma's voice beckoning, "Frans, mekeni! Mangan ta na!"

Vegan Bicol Express
Spicy Squash and Jackfruit Stew in Coconut Milk

Some believe that Bicol Express, a creamy, fiery pork stew, has its origins in a Bicolano vegetable dish called gulay na lada (vegetable with chili peppers). Legend has it, however, that the birthplace of Bicol Express is actually Manila, and that it is named after the train that plies the tracks between the nation's capital and the Bicol region. The recipe below is a vegan version of Francis's mom's original spicy pork belly Bicol Express. He's made some changes by using healthier ingredients, and langka (jackfruit — a widely grown fruit in the Philippines and a widely used meat substitute worldwide) instead of pork. He says the flavor of this dish takes him straight back to childhood!

PREPARATION TIME 50 minutes
YIELD 6 servings

4 tablespoons olive oil
8 cloves garlic, minced
1 large yellow or white onion,
 diced small
2 cups (480 ml) low-sodium vegetable
 stock
3 cups (720 ml) light coconut milk
2 20-oz (600 g) cans young jackfruit,
 rinsed, drained and cut into cubes
2 lbs (900 g) kabocha squash, chopped
 into ½-inch cubes
2 tablespoons vegetarian oyster/stir-fry
 sauce or 4 tablespoons coconut aminos
¼ teaspoon ground black pepper
1 lb (500 g) green beans,
 cut about an inch long
10 Thai bird chilies, sliced on the
 bias (reduce if you don't want the dish
 very spicy)
1 bunch green onions, finely chopped, for
 garnish

1 Heat the oil in a large pan over medium-high heat until it shimmers
2 Add the garlic and onion, stirring. When the onion is transparent, pour in the vegetable stock and coconut milk. Stir. Leave to boil uncovered for about a minute. Lower the heat to medium.
3 Add the jackfruit. Stir then cover. Leave to simmer for about 15 minutes.
4 Stir in the squash, stir-fry sauce or coconut aminos, and pepper.
5 Simmer uncovered for about 10 to 15 minutes or until the liquid is reduced by half, stirring once in a while.
6 Stir in the green beans and the chili. Turn the heat to low. Simmer, covered, for another 10 minutes, or until the beans are the desired texture.
7 Garnish with the green onion and serve with half a cup of cooked rice per serving.

PER SERVING WITH RICE CALORIES
420KCAL | FATS 21.17G
SATURATED FAT 5.37G | **PROTEIN** 9.45G
CARBOHYDRATES 51.34G | **FIBER** 6.63G
SODIUM 524MG | **SUGARS** 10.86G

Bicol Express (1955)

Food, Dreams and Rock 'n' Roll

Mario Llorente Babol

Mario Llorente Babol is a chef and guitar player. He worked in restaurants in Spain and the US before taking a job as head chef on a private yacht. His band, The Balingkitan All Stars, held yearly mini-concerts to support a foundation in the Philippines for children with special needs.

Mario Llorente Babol

> "My parents [...] had to endure backbreaking labor to put me and my siblings through school [...]. They tempered me inside and outside to survive even the toughest of grinds."

I raised the back of my hand to my forehead to wipe off the perspiration beading my skin. Loading sauce-smeared plates into the dishwasher to the nonstop beat of water sloshing from the faucet spray, a Filipino song played in my head: *Planting rice is never fun*. I couldn't agree more. I had firsthand experience of planting rice and I knew it was hard. But compared to washing piles of dirty dishes in Spain? Planting rice seemed like a picnic!

I took the big leap to move to Barcelona, Spain in 2007. Many people think that Filipinos can easily adapt to life in Spain because of our colonial ties to that country. I disagree. When one migrates to Spain armed with a vocabulary of no more than "si" or "no," it's hard to find employment. Landing a job — any job — even washing dishes in my case, is something to be grateful for. Luckily, I'm no stranger to hard work. My parents, who had to endure backbreaking labor to put me and my siblings through school, made sure of that. They tempered me inside and outside to survive even the toughest of grinds.

I was born in Nabua Camarines Sur in Bicol, which makes me an Oragon by birth. By Oragon, I mean a descendant of the indigenous inhabitants of Bicol, known for their warrior-like fierceness and strength, and noble integrity and honor. The word "Oragon" has picked up many different connotations through the years, both positive and negative. But I like to use the word to evoke the ethos of my origin: a battle cry to never give up, never lose hope.

> "When I cook, I hear the rollicking rhythm of rock 'n' roll from knives that slice and dice, from pots and pans that clink and clank, from broths that plip and plop, from oil that splitter-splatters. Together they make a band playing harmoniously to create a flavorful dish."

Back home, my father is a farmer, also known for his culinary and musical prowess; aside from planting rice and growing crops, he also cooks for a living and has won several amateur singing contests. When I was eight years old, my father taught me how to cook rice the traditional way — using firewood! It was a gargantuan task. While waiting for the rice to cook, my father would start strumming his guitar and teach me how to play it. From then on, I would always cook rice while jamming on the guitar.

During my first month in Barcelona, I kept my head down and my blistered hands busy washing dishes. Any job is worth doing well and that's what I did until another turned up — the job was making bocadillos or Spanish-style sandwiches. I didn't even know what bocadillos were until then!

Working ten hours a day, six days a week, I became an expert bocadillo maker. I also learned how to make patatas bravas after peeling sacks and sacks of potatoes. And paella, too, from scratch, and many more dishes. When I cook, I hear the rollicking rhythm of rock 'n' roll — from knives that slice and dice, from pots and pans that clink and clank, from broths that plip and plop, from oil that splitter-splatters. Together they make a band playing harmoniously to create a flavorful dish.

Eventually, I learned how to speak Spanish. I attended culinary school, met influential chefs and cooked at prestigious restaurants. I also made time for my music. Life wouldn't be complete without it.

My career as a chef propelled me to different kinds of kitchens, but sadly none of them were Filipino. Opening my own Filipino restaurant in my new home city remains a dream to be fulfilled; I long to introduce Philippine culture and culinary arts to the locals through a restaurant that I can call my own. Meanwhile, I'm extremely thankful for the opportunities to find outlets for my creativity through food and music.

Food and music are alike in many ways. When I play my guitar, I start by making riffs from basic chords to compose a melody that's in tune. Likewise, in the kitchen, I start with the ingredients and find fresh ways of using them and piecing them together to create a dish that is not only an expression of myself, but something that brings joy to others. Both processes of composition require an elemental understanding of how changing and rearranging basic elements can give a whole new perspective to something familiar. I find this process liberating.

Once again, I evoke Oragon. This time for another of its meanings — someone who excels in anything he does. That, too, is my ongoing dream. To excel at embracing life.

Semi-Vegan Kare-Kare

Roasted Pumpkin and Veggies with Peanut Coconut Sauce

Kare-kare is a stew typically of oxtail, tripe or other beef or pork parts in a rich peanut sauce. The name is an example of the wide use of repeated words in the Filipino language. While the term kare-kare was first used in Pampanga Province to mean an inferior imitation of kari (curry), the exact origin of the dish is uncertain. One theory is that it was first made by sepoys or Indian soldiers serving under the British. They came to Manila on British ships in 1762 to fight the Spanish army. Having won the battle, the British took over Manila for a couple of years, but the sepoys stayed on and intermarried with the locals. Kare-kare is said to be their attempt to abate their yearning for the curry of their homeland using locally available ingredients. Mario gives a Bicolano spin to his flexi-veggie riff on the kare-kare by using coconut water. This recipe can be easily veganized by omitting the bagoong guisado shrimp paste and using vegan peanut butter.

PREPARATION TIME 1 hour
YIELD 6 servings

4 tablespoons olive oil, divided
1 tablespoon annatto seeds
2–4 cloves garlic, crushed
1 sweet onion, fine chopped
2 tablespoons smooth peanut
  butter, reduced fat
½ cup (70 g) rice flour, toasted
2 cups (480 ml) coconut water
2 cups (480 ml) low-sodium vegetable
  broth
8 oz (250 g) pumpkin, peeled and sliced
  into quarter-inch thick semicircles
Salt and pepper, for seasoning and
  sprinkling
1 can banana blossom, about 9 oz (280 g)
  drained weight, rinsed and drained
2 medium Asian eggplants, each cut
  into 6 diagonal pieces
8 oz (250 g) bok choy
8 oz (250 g) green beans, cut
  into 2-inch (5-cm) lengths
½ cup (75 g) toasted peanuts, crushed,
  for garnish, optional
1 tablespoon bagoong guisado shrimp
  paste (*non-vegan), for garnish, optional

Make the Kare-Kare Sauce

1 Heat 2 tablespoons of the oil in a pan over medium heat until it shimmers. Add the annatto seeds. When bubbles start to form and the oil turns deep orange, about 3 minutes, strain the seeds and discard. Pour the annatto-flavored oil back into the pan over medium heat. Add the garlic, stirring occasionally for about 1 minute. Add the onion. Turn the heat up to medium high. Stir until the onion turns translucent, about 3 minutes. Add the peanut butter and the rice flour. Stir until you have a well-blended paste.

2 Add the coconut water and the vegetable broth. Stir until the paste dissolves evenly in the liquid. Let it boil then turn the heat down to low, stirring frequently. Simmer for 15–20 minutes. Check the consistency and add a little water if the sauce has become too thick.

Roast the pumpkin, banana blossom, and eggplant

1 Toss the pumpkin in 1 tablespoon of the oil with a pinch of salt and pepper. Heat a skillet or griddle over high heat. Place the pumpkin in the skillet or on the griddle and cook for about 5 minutes, until one side is slightly charred. Flip the pumpkin over and cook for another 5 minutes until roasted and tender.

2 Pat the banana blossom and eggplant with paper towel. Brush with oil and sprinkle with salt and pepper. Using the skillet or griddle over medium heat, roast on both sides until charred and tender, about 5 minutes for the banana blossom and 10 minutes for the eggplant.

Steam the beans and bok choy

1 Place a pot with 1 inch (2.5 cm) of water over high heat. Place the bok choy and green beans in a steaming basket. When the water boils, put the steaming basket in the pot. Cook until the vegetables are tender-crisp and vibrant green, about 3 minutes.

2 Divide the kare-kare sauce between 6 plates. Divide the vegetables and place on top of the sauce. Garnish if you wish with crushed peanuts and serve with brown rice and shrimp paste, if using. Keeps refrigerated for up to 5 days. Reheat before serving.

PER SERVING WITH ½ CUP BROWN RICE
CALORIES 483KCAL | FATS 19.3G
SATURATED FAT 6.2G | PROTEIN 14G
CARBOHYDRATES 68.3G | FIBER 12.2G
SODIUM 466MG | SUGARS 18.6G

In the Genes

Queenie Laforga

Queenie Laforga is a Filipino American born and raised in Oahu, Hawaii. Having battled with diabetes for over twelve years, she recreates healthy versions of childhood-inspired Filipino favorite dishes and writes about them on her website, Queenie's Food Journey.

> *"I spent a lot of time with Grandma in the kitchen. She'd cook anything her heart desired, relying on her senses instead of measuring implements."*

It's 20th April, 2020. Hawaii has confirmed its 580th Covid-19 case and tenth death. Near my home, where I'm sheltering-in-place, I can hear law enforcement officers patrolling Waikiki Beach. Every now and then, a voice booms through a megaphone: *Aloha! The stay-at-home order is in effect. Please do not gather or sit on the beach!*

As a diabetic, I'm already at high risk for cardiovascular disease and stroke, end-stage kidney disease, lower-extremity amputations and blindness. Now, premature death by coronavirus has been added to that list.

Diabetes runs in my family. I watched my dear grandma battle with the disease: the wounds that took so long to heal, the perforated abdomen, the vision that sometimes became blurred and, at the age of forty-nine — a stroke. She lived the rest of her life with the left half of her body paralyzed and passed away at the very young age of fifty-nine. I have inherited Grandma's diabetic gene. And I have also inherited something else — her love of food.

Before her stroke, I spent a lot of time with Grandma in the kitchen. She'd cook anything her heart desired, relying on her senses instead of measuring implements to make dishes taste heavenly. After her stroke, I spent a lot of time with her tending vegetables in the backyard. In the morning, with a pair of scissors, we'd inspect the ampalayas (bitter melons) dangling from the stems of lobed leaves; we'd snip them from the vine as soon as the half-foot gourd had

> ### "[...] making the right food choices opens up more room in my life for joy to gush in, so that life and food can be relished in perfect harmony."

turned a tad lighter green in color. We harvested all sorts of fruits and vegetables: caimito (star apples), mangoes, radishes, lima beans, tomatoes, red onions, as well as alokon (birch flowers), a common ingredient in vegetable stews in the Ilocos region. The harvest would be handed over to Grandpa, who had taken the reins in the cooking department since Grandma's mobility had been impaired. The dish he'd often prepare was pancit, even though it's usually only served on special occasions.

Since the Covid stay-at-home mandate, my husband, three kids and I have come to an agreement that I should be housebound. We drew up a roster, assigning who goes to the grocery store and when. Everyone except me takes turns to go shopping. Everyone takes precautions religiously, donning masks, sanitizing hands and stripping and changing their clothes in the garage before re-entering the house. My husband and kids are painfully aware of how bad it gets when I'm ill and don't take any risks that can compromise my health. As I can't go out, I do a lot of cooking and a lot of eating!

Nothing I can do or eat will reverse my diabetes but eating healthily can help the body fight disease. It's the most I can do to protect myself and to protect my family as much as they protect me. Outside, I may not have the armor to ward off the disease, but inside the house, especially in the kitchen, I have the power to load everyone up with ammunition. Likewise, by laying

the foundation for healthy eating early in my children's regimen, I hope it'll be a habit that'll stick with them for life.

At the stove, I fire up the wok to a sizzle. I rustle up noodles with vegetables. Grandma didn't exactly make the best food choices earlier on in her life, so I am hopeful that if do, I will outlive her. It doesn't mean, however, that I can't enjoy food as much as she did. Oh no! My love of food is much too strong. A healthy lifestyle for me is a happy lifestyle. I know I can't be healthy if I'm not happy. I discover that making the right food choices opens up more room in my life for joy to gush in, so that life and food can be relished in perfect harmony.

Pancit Zucchini Stir-Fried Zoodles

The Philippines has many types of pancit dishes, all made of starchy noodles. Diets high in refined starches are linked to a higher risk of heart disease, diabetes and weight gain. They also cause blood sugars to spike rapidly and then fall sharply — a problem for diabetics like Queenie. To enjoy pancit without worrying about blood sugar levels, she replaces the noodles with zucchini spiralized into noodle-like strands.

PREPARATION TIME 20 minutes
+ 30 minutes soaking time
YIELD 8 servings

1 cup (240 ml) water
4 teaspoons annatto seeds
2 tablespoons extra-virgin olive oil
5 cloves garlic, minced
1 medium onion, thinly sliced
1 lb (500 g) tofu, cut into strips
5 shiitake mushrooms, fresh or dried
   (if using dried, soak in water for at least
   an hour), sliced
4 large zucchini, spiraled or sliced
   skin-on into thin long strips
½ small cabbage, chopped
½ medium red bell pepper, cut into
   thin strips
3 medium carrots, cut into thin strips
3 celery stalks with leaves, thinly
   chopped
2 cups (240 g) green beans, sliced
   diagonally, or snow peas
3 tablespoons low-sodium soy sauce
   or 3 tablespoons coconut aminos
1 low-sodium vegetable stock cube,
   or 3 tablespoons Pinoy Powder (page
   15)
2 scallions, chopped
Fresh ground black pepper to taste
8 calamansi, halved or 2 lemons, cut in
   wedges
2 boiled eggs, sliced (optional,
   *non-vegan)

1 Bring the cup of water to a boil. Remove from the heat and add the annatto seeds. Leave to soak for 30 minutes. Drain and discard the seeds. Set aside the colored water.

2 Preheat a wok or skillet over medium heat. Add the oil. When the oil shimmers, add the garlic and onions. Stir until the garlic turns golden and the onions transparent. Add the tofu and mushrooms and stir-fry for 30 seconds. Add the zucchini, cabbage, bell pepper, carrots, celery and green beans. Turn the heat to high and mix. Pour in the annatto water, soy sauce and stock cube. Stir-fry until the vegetables turn vibrant in color and are tender but still crisp.

3 Top with the scallions, pepper, and eggs if using, and serve with calamansi or lemon.

PER SERVING CALORIES 197KCAL | FATS 11G
SATURATED FAT 2.7G | PROTEIN 13.2G
CARBOHYDRATES 15.6G
FIBER 4.8G | SODIUM 564MG | SUGARS 4.8G

Sizzling Sisig from the Heart

Richgail Enriquez-Diez

Richgail Enriquez-Diez is the author of the cookbook *Filipino Vegan*. Her cooking show on YouTube is called *Astig Vegan Cooking*. Born and raised in the Philippines, she and her family moved to the San Francisco Bay Area when she was fifteen years old.

> *"He and Ma have always been there for me no matter where the wind of change blew."*

When the heart specialist broke the news that Dad needed a triple coronary artery bypass, my family and I were stunned into silence. The procedure, the doctor explained, needed to be done right away. Dad was suffering from severely clogged arteries and each day that passed without treatment posed a risk to his life.

At the time of his diagnosis, Dad was still only in his sixties. He had a crown of thick black hair; his circumflex-shaped brows accented eyes that when opened, mirrored the goodness of his heart. His broad shoulders had always carried our family's burdens with strength.

He and Ma have always been there for me no matter where the winds of change blew. Like when I was eighteen and wanted to pursue broadcast journalism far from home. Dad and Ma didn't stand in my way. Although it saddened them to see me move away, they helped me pack my bags and hauled them with me from San Francisco to Bend, Oregon. A year later, I changed my mind and decided to pursue something else instead. Again, Dad and Ma supported my decision without question and traveled back to Oregon to pick me up.

A time also came when I ventured into acting. My parents made the effort to attend each one of my plays. They sat in the front row, beaming with pride and applauding my performance regardless of whether I was portraying a grandma or a show girl.

> **"In honor of Dad and Ma, I developed a recipe veganizing the famous, pork-heavy sisig without burdening it with too much sodium. It is an enduring expression of gratitude to my parents for a lifetime of unconditional love and unwavering support for their unconventional daughter."**

Then the time came when I decided to become vegan. Veganism was quite unheard of in my family. We had been raised eating Filipino food, which is notable for the wide use of animal-based ingredients, even in vegetable dishes. Sisig, for instance, the popular Filipino dish Anthony Bourdain said was "perfectly positioned to win the hearts and mind of the world," couldn't be meat heavier.

Yes, our family has always loved and lived on a predominantly carnivorous diet. Dad was no exception to this. He enjoyed meat lavishly seasoned with sodium and oozing with fat. Therefore, my resolve to eat an exclusively plant-based diet must have seemed like a sharp turn. But my parents are supportive, bragging about me and proudly pointing me out as the "vegan one" at family parties. They urge relatives to watch my cooking shows on YouTube and have even appeared as my special guests in a couple of my video episodes.

Dad survived a long and invasive heart procedure. Before he was discharged from the hospital, his doctor issued him with strict instructions to follow a low-salt diet. Although he wasn't too happy about that, my dad understood and conceded. Ma, too, because of her high blood pressure, was advised by her doctors to be more mindful of her salt intake. Alas, they're not the only ones who suffer from these conditions at a young age. Some of my aunts and uncles have also been dealing with health problems since they hit their sixties, and for many people these problems begin even earlier.

In honor of Dad and Ma, I've developed a recipe veganizing the famous, pork-heavy sisig without burdening it with too much sodium. It is an enduring expression of gratitude to my parents for a lifetime of unconditional love and unwavering support for their unconventional daughter.

Vegan Sisig Mushroom and Tofu Hash

Sisig was first described in a 1732 dictionary of the Kapampangan language as a salad of tart green fruits, such as guava or papaya, dressed with salt, pepper, garlic and vinegar. But the sisig everyone knows today is made from parts of a pig head, usually served sizzling on a cast-iron plate. Pig head sisig takes at least three hours to cook. This vegan dish can be made in twenty minutes or less and mimics the taste and texture of the meat dish, especially if you use high-quality, extra-firm tofu.

PREPARATION TIME 20 minutes
YIELD 4 servings

2 tablespoons white vinegar
1 tablespoon low-sodium soy sauce
  or coconut aminos
1 teaspoon organic brown sugar*
  or coconut sugar
½ teaspoon freshly ground black
  pepper
1–2 Thai chilies, minced (or more
  for extra kick)
5 oz (150 g) oyster mushrooms,
  diced small
5 oz (150 g) trumpet mushrooms,
  diced small
5 oz (150 g) beech mushrooms,
  diced small
4–5 tablespoons sunflower oil
1 block firm tofu, about 8 oz (250 g),
  diced
3 large cloves garlic, minced
1 small yellow onion, diced
1 teaspoon calamansi juice
  or lemon or lime juice

PER SERVING CALORIES 321KCAL
FATS 23.5G | SATURATED FAT 2.8G
PROTEIN 16.4G
CARBOHYDRATES 16.1G | FIBER 6G
SODIUM 160MG | SUGARS 3.9G
* In the US, conventional brown sugar is
not vegan because it uses animal bone
char in the refining process. Organic
brown sugar is vegan.

1 In a small bowl, combine the vinegar, soy sauce, sugar, pepper and chili. Add the mushrooms and mix thoroughly.
2 In a frying pan, heat the oil over medium heat until it shimmers. Add the tofu and fry until golden on all sides.
3 Add the garlic and onions to the frying pan with the tofu. Lower the heat to medium low and sauté for one minute or until the garlic and onions are fragrant.
4 Mix in the marinated mushrooms and sauce from Step 1. Turn the heat to medium high and cook until the mushrooms are tender, about five minutes.
5 Add the calamansi juice and mix. Taste and adjust the seasoning.
6 Remove from the heat and serve hot.

OPTION
You can use other kinds of mushrooms, such as white button, portobello or shiitake.

CHAPTER 6

Lamandagat

Seafood Delights

Filipino meals consist of rice and ulam (a dish served with rice).
It is not uncommon to have at least two kinds of ulam per meal,
one of which would most likely be of fish or seafood. The Philippine
archipelago is made up of over seven thousand islands scattered
between the South China Sea and the Pacific Ocean, where marine
life abounds. As a result, fish and its derivatives are a key source of
protein in the Filipino diet.

Ironically, even though fish is an everyday food, in our mainly
Catholic population there has also been a long tradition of eating
fish on Friday, when we abstain from meat. These days, this tradition
is mainly confined to Fridays that fall during Lent.

Recipes in this chapter are closely in line with the 2019
American Heart Health program, which recommends that a
main dish should contain no more than 600 mg of sodium,
500 calories and 2 teaspoons of added sugars per serving.

Finding Magic in Iceland

Jennifer Fergesen

Jennifer Fergesen is an American food journalist of Filipino and Nordic descent. Her project, The Global Carinderia (www.globalcarinderia.com), a series of essays that profiles Filipino restaurants around the world to showcase the diversity of the global diaspora, has received multiple awards.

"There are few places left where magic is real [...] Iceland is one. The Philippines is another."

"Magic is real in Iceland," the American in Stúdentakjallarinn told me.

Stúdentakjallarinn is the campus pub of the University of Iceland, where college IDs get you half-price Carlsbergs. Straining over the squall of Nordic metal on the speakers, the American yelled a summary of his doctorate: a study of Icelanders' connection to the supernatural.

"There are few places left where magic is real," he continued. "Iceland is one. The Philippines is another."

I must have looked surprised then, more than I had at the mention of magic. I'd said nothing about my connection to the Philippines. Could he have seen it from the shape of my features, the color of my skin? Few can, even among the Filipino immigrants I was there to interview.

Filipinos make up the largest non-European immigrant group in Iceland: some 2,000 people in a country of 360,000. They work in all the gaps Iceland's sparse population leaves open in its growing economy. For nearly two years of visits, I circumnavigated the country looking for them.

I followed listings of lumpia and adobo on otherwise amorphous menus — kabayan (compatriot) calling cards — and traveled to meet the Filipino restaurateurs behind them. In Reykjavík, I met a pair of hotel cooks who run an underground catering company called Pinoy Taste on Facebook, where they hawk everything from malunggay (Moringa) pandesal to Pampanga-style longanisa. Hours north, in the village of Borgarnes, I interviewed a woman

> **"The Filipino-Icelandic dish that will linger the longest in my memory, however, the one that plays at the corners of my tongue even now, is escabeche. I made it from Atlantic cod, a gift from some fishermen I met at the town pool."**

who fled post-Marcos Philippines and now owns a restaurant, slinging pancit alongside beef stroganoff and burgers.

I'd enter someone's home with a notepad and ten questions and leave with my arms full of smuggled Skyflakes crackers or borrowed books, sure I'd made a friend for life. I was as star-struck as if I had been interviewing celebrities instead of local restaurateurs.

But it was in Skagaströnd that I learned the most about what it means to be Filipino in Iceland. I settled down in an artist residency in that far-north village, some thirty miles (50 km) below the Arctic Circle, to write the essays that would become The Global Carinderia. Skagaströnd contained no restaurants — only a small grocery store and a gas station with a burger grill in the back.

So I cooked for myself. It was a welcome change after months of near-nonstop traveling, a break from hot dogs and convenience-store sandwiches thick with mayonnaise. I remembered something one of the owners of Pinoy Taste had told me. "Filipinos have to have Filipino food," she said. "It's in our blood."

The grocery store had one dusty shelf marked "Austurlenskur" (Oriental), stocked with soy sauce, dry noodles and not much else. Like generations of diasporic cooks before me, I learned to make do. I worked sweet potatoes and potato starch into a sticky simulacrum of carioca, shredded turnip in place of papaya for Ilocos-style empanadas, then foisted my inventions on Skagaströnders and my fellow foreign artists. The

mayor said my empanadas were the first she ever tasted.

The Filipino-Icelandic dish that will linger the longest in my memory, however, the one that plays at the corners of my tongue even now, is escabeche. I made it from Atlantic cod, a gift from some fishermen I met at the town pool.

I got the idea to make escabeche from Marvi Gil, a psychiatric nurse and writer who moved to Iceland from the Philippines in 2008. The dish suits the Icelandic palate, she told me; their taste for soured seafood rivals even that of the Filipinos, whose kinilaw and paksiw pale in comparison to hákarl (fermented shark) and súr hvalur (pickled whale). It is also one of the few items in the Filipino repertoire that requires no substitute ingredients when made in Iceland. Vinegar and sugar you can find anywhere, and the geothermal greenhouses grow excellent peppers.

If there is magic in Iceland, I felt it the day I served that escabeche to my new friends in Skagaströnd. I've felt the same in the Philippines, around tables that groaned with all the small luxuries the hosts could gather, around beachside bonfires thrumming with impromptu songs. I felt it, too, in the homes of the Filipino expats who welcomed me into their Icelandic lives. Anyone can open themselves this way, but few places ingrain it into their customs. Iceland is one. The Philippines is another.

Baked Escabeche Sweet and Sour Cod

Escabeche harks back to a Persian dish called al-sikbaj, which was brought by the Arabs to Spain in the eighth century. The Spanish spread it to their colonized territories, including the Philippines. Traditionally in this Catholic country, housework was prohibited on Good Friday. Escabeche — fish marinated in seasoned vinegar — met the need to prepare Good Friday food at least a day ahead. Spanish-style escabeche cooks fish in vinegar, while its Filipino-Chinese counterpart adds sweet-and-sour sauce to fried fish. Jennifer gives the Filipino escabeche a heart-healthy spin by baking the fish instead of frying it.

PREPARATION TIME 30 minutes
YIELD 4 servings

FOR THE FISH
1 cup (100 g) panko breadcrumbs
½ teaspoon garlic powder
¼ teaspoon salt
¼ teaspoon ground black pepper
1 egg white
4 cod fillets, 5 oz (150 g) each
1 tablespoon olive oil or cooking spray

FOR THE SAUCE
2½ tablespoons sugar
¼ cup (60 ml) apple cider vinegar
½ low-sodium bouillon cube, or 1
  tablespoon Pinoy Powder (page 15),
  mixed in ½ cup (120 ml) warm water
1 tablespoon cornstarch
Pepper, to taste, divided
1 tablespoon olive oil
1 onion, halved and thinly sliced
2 cloves garlic, minced
1-inch (2.5-cm) piece ginger, minced
1 red bell pepper, thinly sliced
1 orange, yellow or green
  bell pepper, thinly sliced

GARNISH
½ cup (10 g) parsley or cilantro,
  chopped
¼ cup (25 g) scallions, chopped

PER SERVING WITH ½ CUP RICE **CALORIES** 497KCAL | FATS 9.4G | SATURATED FAT 1.2G PROTEIN 47.3G | CARBOHYDRATES 52.8G FIBER 2.9G | SODIUM 520MG | SUGARS 10.6G

Make the fish

1 Preheat the oven to 425°F (220°C). Line a baking sheet with a silicone baking mat or parchment paper.
2 In a shallow bowl, combine the breadcrumbs, garlic powder, salt and pepper. In another bowl, whisk the egg white with 1 teaspoon water. Dip the cod fillets into the egg-white mixture, then coat in the breadcrumb mixture. Place the fish on the prepared baking sheet. Brush the tops of the fillets with the olive oil or spray with cooking spray. Bake for 10 minutes, turn, then bake for a further 5–10 minutes or until the fish is golden-brown and cooked through.

Make the sauce

1 In a bowl, whisk together the sugar, vinegar, bouillon broth, cornstarch and a pinch of pepper until the sugar and the cornstarch are dissolved. Set aside.
2 In a skillet or wok, heat the olive oil over medium-high heat until it shimmers. Add the onion and cook until translucent, then add the garlic and ginger, stirring for about 30 seconds. When the garlic softens and turns slightly golden, add the bell peppers and stir until they brighten up in color and are crisp-tender, about 1–2 minutes. Lower the heat and pour in the sauce mixture from Step 1, stirring briskly until it thickens. Turn off heat and add pepper to taste.
3 Place the baked fish onto a serving plate and pour the sauce over. Garnish with the chopped parsley or cilantro and the scallions.

Extracting the Milk of Life

Marvin Braceros

Marvin Braceros is an Italian-trained Filipino chef specializing in Filipino and Italian cuisines. His gourmet restaurant in Milan, Yum – Taste of the Philippines, has been on Gambero Rosso's list of best restaurants in Italy for three consecutive years. He has also opened restaurants in the Philippines and Malta.

> "I was a foreign worker juggling three jobs as a dishwasher, window cleaner and domestic helper, in a land where people spoke a language I could barely understand."

I shook the water off my calloused hands in the sink and glanced around to admire the fruits of my labor. The toilet, immaculately white, dazzled. The mirror, washed and wiped until spotless, spoke the truth — perhaps quite brutally — about how my work has taken its toll on my body.

There I was, standing out like a sore thumb. Not because I thought a college graduate and former airline ground steward like me was too good to be cleaning the bathrooms of other people. Nor was it because I was a foreign worker juggling three jobs as a dishwasher, window cleaner and domestic helper, in a land where people spoke a language I could barely understand. It wasn't because I was what is called in Italian a "clandestino"; in Tagalog, "TNT" for tago ng tago (always in hiding); or in English, an illegal alien, at a time when anti-immigrant sentiment was starting to percolate in the country.

No, the reason I stood out like a sore thumb was my physical appearance: a man who stood in stark contrast to the room he had just painstakingly scrubbed to a sparkle. Shadows hollowed out his eye sockets and cheeks. A stubble, by no means designer, was creeping over his face.

The sight of my reflection prompted an unwelcome yet familiar thought to sneak into my head. It taunted and jeered: *Bravo, Marvin! Enjoy! Coz this same shit you're doing today? You'll be doing it again tomorrow, the day after tomorrow and the day after that.* I kicked the thought out of my

> **"I don't want to spend my life always chasing the next big thing to feel content. Joy can emanate even from the most menial of tasks if you let it. Like extracting milk from a coconut — sometimes, it's not what is extracted in the end that counts, but what is extracted from the process."**

mind. Self-pride, not self-pity, eventually won the day. I smiled at the man in the mirror. *Hey, dude! Hang in there. You're doing an excellent job!*

The heady aroma of tomato sauce developing flavor slipped in through a crack in the door. It could beckon a growl from the stomach even if it wasn't empty. I bolted to the kitchen fearing that the sauce I left gently simmering on the stove had stuck to the bottom of the pot.

Oil from the tomato base oozed and floated on top of the reduced sauce. I stirred the bubbling sugo di pomodoro reminding myself how lucky I was. I lived in Milan, considered by many as the planet's fashion capital! I was in a country known to have one of the finest culinary traditions in the world and I had access to some of the most delicious food on earth! Imagine what frontiers could open up to me if I had a culinary degree from one of the prestigious schools of gastronomy in the city? Imagine what novelty I could offer if I could bring food from my home country and marry it with the cooking techniques and fresh produce of Italy?

***

It took five years before my status in Italy was legalized, thanks to an amnesty program. If I had known when I arrived that it was going to take that long, I don't know if I would have lasted. Instead, by living moment by moment, the time whizzed past like a breeze. Sure, I was happy for the great jobs I managed to land as chef at Dolce & Gabbana and at Martini. Yes, I was over the moon when the gourmet Filipino restaurant I owned received recognition. And true, I was ecstatic when, following the success of my restaurant in Milan, I opened more restaurants in Manila and Malta. Yet, I don't want to spend my life always chasing the next big thing to feel content. Joy can emanate even from the most menial of tasks if you let it. Like extracting milk from a coconut — sometimes, it's not what is extracted in the end that counts, but what is extracted from the process. Admittedly, it's more convenient to buy store-bought coconut milk and, often, the taste is not far off from the freshly pressed liquid. But every now and then, I like to go to great lengths. I cup a perfect sphere-shaped coconut with my hands, feel the little bristles of fiber jutting out from its shell tickle my palms, hear the sploshing of liquid as I shake and drain it before whacking it open, see the unraveling of its shimmering white flesh, grate it, squeeze it and watch the milk seep out through my clenched fist. It's peace. It's joy.

Ginataang Sinaing
Banana Blossom–Wrapped Salmon and Green Papaya in Coconut Milk

This dish is a riff on ginataang sinaing na tulingan (coconut braised mackerel), popular in the coastal areas of Batangas. Salmon, tilapia, trout or sea bass can work well in this dish in place of mackerel. Some people like to cook the fish wrapped in banana leaves for the additional flavor it imparts. Marvin suggests using banana blossom petals, which are chock-full of essential nutrients for good heart health. Green papaya is added as a vegetable for good measure.

PER SERVING CALORIES 496KCAL | FATS 20.8G
SATURATED FAT 7G | PROTEIN 67.4G
CARBOHYDRATES 6.6G | FIBER 2.2G
SODIUM 378.3MG | SUGARS 2.3G

PREPARATION TIME 20 minutes
YIELD 6 servings

20-oz (600 g) can banana blossom in brine, rinsed and drained
6 salmon fillets, each 3–4 oz (100 g)
1 medium-sized white onion
14-oz (400 ml) can light coconut milk
1 small green papaya, peeled, seeded and chopped into 1-inch (2.5-cm) wedges, or large zucchini, chopped into 1-inch semicircles
½ cup (120 ml) water
2 teaspoons canola oil
Pinch of salt and pepper

1 Set aside 6–12 banana blossom petals. Finely slice the rest.
2 Roll each salmon fillet in one or two petals. Set aside.
3 Heat the oil in a 9-inch (23-cm) pan over medium heat until it shimmers. Add the onion and stir until translucent and limp. Stir in the coconut milk, green papaya and remaining banana blossom.
4 Add the water and cook for 3 minutes, stirring occasionally. Drop the wrapped salmon into the mixture and simmer for 3 to 5 minutes or until the salmon is cooked to your taste. Season with salt and pepper.
5 Serve hot. Pairs best with rice.

Setting the Table

Will Mordido

Pangasinan-born Will Mordido moved to New Zealand with his family at age five. He won silver at the international Jeunes Chefs Rôtisseurs competition and became the country's first ever representative at the finals of the world chef championship, the Bocuse d'Or. He started Buko, a pop-up restaurant that celebrates Filipino flavors.

It's a Tuesday at a Pacific Rim-ish inspired restaurant in Auckland, the equivalent of a Monday to a "regular" nine-to-five working person. For a sous chef like me, it means my prep list is long, the morning deliveries are on their way and lots of emails have to be written and phone follow-ups made to ensure the team's work flow is not disturbed.

We're inching closer and closer to lunch service sorting through our mise en place and more, when the head chef announces out of the blue, "We're putting on a special today." A collective sigh of stress echoes in the kitchen, yet, we carry on and comply, "Yes, Chef!"

I rush back to the stove to turn off the heat under the largest pot in the kitchen; my salmon sinigang stock for a risotto has been simmering since we got in. I grab the commis chef by the arm and hand him a tea towel to protect against the hot handle.

"Come help me with this pot, let's strain it and get it out of the way."

"Yes, Chef!" he says, to which I reply, "Will, call me Will, I don't like being called Chef." He smiles as he takes the scalding stock out back, past the head chef who had just screamed at him earlier like the restaurant was on fire.

A waitress comes to the kitchen with coffee for the team, a sure sign that she's about to ask "Can you please help me move a few tables outside? We are almost ready to open."

Unlike most chefs, I don't drink coffee, but I hop along to help her with the tables while my head is busy thinking of tasks left unticked on

> *"'Yes, Chef!'*
> *he says, to which I reply,*
> *'Will, call me Will,*
> *I don't like being called Chef.'"*

> ## "I shall not let my dream of owning a restaurant get in the way of finding joy. [...] True happiness comes not from external achievements, but from one's inner self."

my checklist. Come to think of it, setting tables was my first foray into the world of gastronomy. When I was little, Mum would cook dishes she was accustomed to eating in her home province of Pangasinan. My favorite was balatong, aka monggo or mung bean. I'd offer to help Mum in the kitchen, but she'd only entrust me with the humble task of setting the table. While my hands set the spoons and forks down, my head was somewhere else — in the kitchen, where a pot of balatong simmered.

At twelve o'clock on the dot, our first set of diners storm in. The order machine churns out docket after docket.

"Behind! Hot tray!" a chef exclaims. "Legs! Oven, please!" another yells as he reaches deep into the oven with tongs to fetch a tray of beef steak, seconds from being overcooked. Careful to navigate away from the hot rack and avoid additional battle scars, he places the tray of beef next to me, ready to be plated and met with lashings of adobo flavored jus.

Drenched in sweat, making it look like we'd swum across the Tasman Sea, we reach the finish line. The deluge of dockets subsides, well, at least for the first half of the day. We rinse and repeat for dinner.

At home past midnight, after working for twelve hours or more, relaxing in front of the TV I wonder if this is all worth it. Over the years, I've lost weight, not because I wanted to. Bits and pieces I taste here and there when I'm quality checking are usually my first meal of the day. Stress is a constant undercurrent in my life. Every

day is the same: wake up, go to work, work. I consider it lucky if I get to see my family twice a week. It's not the way to live.

***

I've taken a break. After a year or so away from the heat of à la carte, I am hungry to get back in. I've been taking my time to enjoy the little things in life. I am healthier. I am happier. As for the restaurant world, I am nearing my goal of a permanent home for Buko, my Filipino pop-up restaurant. Whenever and wherever that may be, one thing is for sure: I shall not let my ambition of owning a restaurant get in the way of finding joy. I know now that true happiness comes not from external achievements, but from one's inner self.

As for Mum's balatong, it'll be on the menu with a splash of me weaved through it, and this time, I'll make sure I'm fully present, body and mind, even if I'm just setting the table. No task is too mundane to be performed as merely a means to an end; we should look for the joy in everything we do.

Balatong at Lamandagat
Sautéed Mung Beans with Seared Snapper and Prawn

The balatong recipe made by Will's mum, Fe, uses pork fat, fermented fish sauce and ampalaya (bitter melon) leaves. In this version, Will replaces these ingredients with olive oil, seafood and fish sauce, and celery. He prepared a similar dish for a dinner for Jacinda Ardern when she was prime minister of New Zealand.

PREPARATION TIME 1 hour +
 soaking overnight
YIELD 4 servings

2 tablespoons olive oil, divided
5 cloves garlic, finely chopped
1 onion, finely diced
2-inch (5-cm) piece fresh ginger,
 peeled and grated
1 cup (200 g) dried mung beans,
 rinsed and soaked in salted water
 overnight, then rinsed and drained
2 cups (480 ml) water
4 medium to large-sized raw prawns,
 shell and head on
4 celery stalks, finely chopped
2½ teaspoons fish sauce
Pinch of freshly ground white pepper
 to taste
4 oz (120 g) spinach, washed and
 roughly chopped
4 fresh snapper fillets (or other firm
 white fish fillets)
Salt, for seasoning

OPTION
You can swap garlic, onion and celery for 5 Guisa Ice Cubes (see page 17).

PER SERVING CALORIES 344KCAL
FATS 10.1G | SATURATED FAT 1.7G
PROTEIN 53.1G
CARBOHYDRATES 8.6G | FIBER 2.5G
SODIUM 572MG | SUGARS 3.2G

1 Heat half the oil in a large saucepan over medium heat until it shimmers. Add the garlic and stir until fragrant. Add the onion and stir until translucent. Add the ginger and stir for 2–3 minutes. Add the mung beans, stir for 1–2 minutes, then add the water and bring to a boil. Lower the heat to medium and let simmer, stirring frequently to prevent burning. Cook for 30–40 minutes until the mung beans are tender.

2 Add the prawns and celery to the saucepan and stir for 3 minutes or until the prawns are cooked. Add the fish sauce, pepper and spinach. Remove from heat and keep covered.

3 Season the fish with the salt. Heat 1 tablespoon of the oil in a large nonstick pan until it shimmers. Sear the fish, skin side down, until golden brown then turn to finish cooking. Drain excess oil on a plate lined with paper towels. Divide the mung beans and prawns into bowls and top with the fish fillets. Serve with half a cup of steamed rice per serving.

The Heart Always Remembers

Amormia Orino

Of Bicolano roots, 2022 James Beard Award semi-finalist Amormia Orino started hosting pop-up restaurants when she moved from Virginia to Atlanta in 2018. Her popular Kamayan pop-ups have won her awards and media coverage. She took part in a PBS documentary about food in Atlanta and the South and is a contributor to the book *Fearless Innovation: Atlanta's Food Story*.

> *"I've always adored Mama. I'm the bunso, the youngest of six. I followed her everywhere like a shadow. I would watch her in the kitchen always humming and singing while she cooked."*

A loud thump came from downstairs where my mom's room was. I flew down the staircase thinking she had fallen. At eighty-two, she would sometimes lose her balance. I switched on the lights and discovered the room in disarray: a lamp toppled from the bedside table; sheets tangled; and my mom sitting on the floor staring at her hands. When she looked up, frustration, confusion then embarrassment flashed across her face in quick succession. I asked her if she'd had a nightmare. She looked back at me, eyebrows drawn together and one hand scratching her temple. I tried to hide my fear and the struggle to comprehend what was happening. I waited for her to speak up. She'd been having difficulties with word retrieval since she arrived in Hawaii from Manila. *Perhaps she was just jet-lagged*. But I knew I was in denial.

It could be dementia.

It is dementia.

If you know my mama, you'd say, "No way!" She's feisty, a force to reckon with, fiercely independent. Even at the age of eighty-two, she traveled halfway around the world by herself. We bought her a walking cane but she hated using it. She would hide it from view whenever we took pictures of her.

I've always adored Mama. I'm the bunso, the youngest — of six children. I followed her everywhere like a shadow. I would watch her in the kitchen always humming and singing while

> **"Cooking was always her passion — her love language. It never was mine. I never cooked. But one day, I just decided to pick up a wok, a pound of crabs and a can of coconut milk. Boy, was it a revelation! [...] I found it cathartic. Healing."**

she cooked. I never had a contentious relationship with her. Even when we were thousands of miles apart, or even when she was away for years, once she landed, we were always able to pick up exactly where we left off.

One thing I never did was discuss my own problems with her. I never told her when I was going through heartbreak. I wanted the times with Mama to be happy. I wanted them to be about her.

Now and then she'd say it worried her that I was childless, "Amormia, paano na pag tanda mo?" (Amormia, how's it going to be when you get old?) I'd brush it off and tell her, "Ang wrinkles mader. That's why I eat quinoa and do Pilates, and when the time comes I'll hire someone to change my diaper."

That's my only regret. That I never cried on her shoulder. That I never admitted that we never stop needing our mothers.

✳ ✳ ✳

Mama is eighty-five now. Her cognitive grip on life is slipping away. She's disappearing. Vanishing. The once animated octogenarian, who laughed so loudly while telling stories no longer speaks. Her gaze is empty.

She's still here. But she's not. The grief that chokes me as I try to come to terms with this is overwhelming. The pain is all-consuming. I wake up in the middle of the night and I feel it in every breath. I wonder if she's lonely. I wonder if she feels the rage I feel. The helplessness.

My mom can no longer comfort me. I've had to find a way to distract myself from my obsessive thoughts of her imminent passing.

Cooking was always her passion — her love language. It was never mine. I never cooked. But one day, I just decided to pick up a wok, a pound of crabs and a can of coconut milk. Boy, was it a revelation! Though I didn't burst into song the way she used to, I found it cathartic. Healing. Cooking evokes memories of my childhood, of Mama still strong and preparing meals for us. And with every dish I cook from memory, I get closer to accepting that while Mama's brain no longer remembers me, I'm certain her heart does. It gives me peace to know that I am always in her heart and she in mine.

Ginataang Alimasag
Coconut-Stewed Crab with Squash, Tofu and Moringa

Though crab is naturally high in sodium, it is low in calories and saturated fat and rich in protein, minerals and Vitamin B_{12}. Amormia describes this dish as being as comforting as a warm hug from her parents. Coconut milk and bird's eye chili — both from the province of Bicol — are staples in her pantry. This recipe uses squash and Moringa leaves but any other vegetable, such as eggplant or spinach, would work. Blues are her crab of choice but feel free to use the type of crab you prefer. To clean crabs, run in cold water and scrub off dirt or grime with a kitchen brush.

PER SERVING CALORIES 226KCAL | FATS 15.4G
SATURATED FAT 7.1G PROTEIN 13.5G
CARBOHYDRATES 11.6G | FIBER 3.4G
SODIUM 159MG SUGARS 4.5G

PREPARATION TIME 40 minutes
YIELD 4 servings

1 tablespoon canola or safflower oil
1 tablespoon minced garlic
2 tablespoons diced yellow onion
2 tablespoons minced fresh ginger
14-oz (400-ml) can light coconut milk
2 bird's eye chilies, minced
3 tablespoons coconut aminos
4 blue crabs, about 1 lb (500 g) total, cleaned and
  cut in half
1 lb (500 g) kabocha or
  calabaza squash, cut into cubes
6 oz (200 g) firm tofu, cut into cubes
1 cup (30 g) Moringa leaves or any leafy vegetable
Freshly ground black pepper, to taste

1 Heat the oil in a large saucepan over medium heat. Add the garlic, stirring regularly until it begins to brown, about 2 minutes.
2 Add the onion and ginger. Sauté until the onion is caramelized.
3 Add the coconut milk, bird's eye chilies and coconut aminos. Turn the heat to high and bring the pan to a boil.
4 Add the crabs and reduce the heat. Simmer for 10 minutes. Add the squash and cook for another 8–10 minutes. Add the tofu and Moringa leaves and simmer for 5 minutes.
5 Turn off the heat and season with freshly ground black pepper.

The Vessel

Jeremy Villanueva

Jeremy Villanueva is the executive chef of Romulo Café, a Filipino restaurant named Second Most Loved Local Restaurant in London by _Time Out_. Jeremy has worked at various renowned restaurants, including UK celebrity chef Tony Tobin's La Poste; he has also worked as chef for Holland America Cruises.

In 2009 in Seattle, Washington, I boarded a cruise headed for Alaska. The vessel was as imposing as it was grand. Spanning almost a mile, it could accommodate about 1500 guests and a crew of over 600. There was a great hustle and bustle as the crew boarded, collected their uniforms and reported to their stations.

I was shown to the kitchen of a fine dining restaurant serving up to 160 guests daily. It was workplace culture shock to say the least. The grind, seven days a week, started at eight in the morning and continued until ten thirty at night or sometimes one or two in the morning. There was constant cleaning, and inspections at all hours. Standing for at least twelve hours a day on a teetering vessel took a bit of getting used to. Labor was split along the lines of ethnicity; there wasn't a lot of general mixing. The drudgery was exacerbated by loneliness at being far from my family and by the huge effort I had to make to try and fit into the ship's system.

A saving grace was that the kitchen was predominantly Filipino. I met Filipinos from practically every corner of the "old country," from Aparri to Jolo. Each had with them their own stories, their own language, and one of the favorite topics (being chefs, of course) was their regional cuisine.

To break the monotony of staff food, a lot of us would cook our regional dishes and serve these up as a late dinner or as pulutan nibbles to go with the occasional drinking sessions to wind down after work. Depending on who was given

> _"Each had with them their own stories, their own languages and one of the favorite topics (being chefs, of course) was their regional cuisine."_

> ## "To break the monotony of staff food, a lot of us would cook our regional dishes. [...] The camaraderie created from a shared love of Filipino food helped me through a very difficult time."

the task of cooking, it could be Ilocos-style miki noodle soup one night and Batangas-style beef mami noodles the next. The ingenuity of the chefs in getting their ingredients on board deserved a standing ovation. The camaraderie created from a shared love of Filipino food helped me through a very difficult time.

The route of the last couple of cruises before the end of my contract took us south to warmer climes. We cruised from San Francisco to Hawaii. Goodbye glaciers, hello sandy beaches! Through a combination of bribes, favors and downright begging, I managed to get shore leave. As we arrived off the coast, the smell of the salty breeze hit me. It was a smell I was familiar with. I could've been in the Philippines!

I took the chance to laze on the beach, taking in the sights and sounds, casting my mind back to the last time I was on a beach, at home in the Philippines. In 2016, my family and I took an excursion to the northwest of Luzon. At a beach in Ilocos, the wives of fishermen had asked if we wanted them to cook fish for us. It was an interesting offer and an absolute bargain.

The cooking was simple home cooking but the freshness of the ingredients spoke for itself and could not have benefited more from the humble accompaniment of plain boiled rice cooked over embers of coconut husks. First we were served pinangat na sap-sap (flat fish in broth) which we sipped as we waited for the rest of the dishes. Then as the rice arrived, more varieties of the catch of the day followed, reminding me of how simple and soul-satisfying Filipino food can be.

Squid prepared in two ways was the last dish to be served. The tentacles and ink, cooked adobo style, shimmered in its jet-black sauce. The squid's body, grilled to a char, was stuffed with onions, tomatoes, queso puti (fresh cheese) and kamias (Averrhoa bilimbi, a sour fruit). This would inspire me to create a dish years later that would appear on the menu of Romulo.

My shipmates called me to head back. Suddenly, I was aware of the greasy smell of burgers and fries being cooked at nearby eateries. The sensory pictures I had painted in the corners of my mind as I enjoyed the warm rays of the sun, the cool breeze and the crashing of waves dissipated. As the reality of a few more weeks of hard labor loomed, I boarded the ship, wishing it could take me home. To me, the Philippines — even after all these years living in the West — is still a place I call home. One day . . .

Rellenong Pusit
Squid Stuffed with Tomatoes and White Cheese

Relleno-style or stuffed dishes traditionally entail multiple complicated steps and a wide assortment of ingredients. Luckily, this rellenong pusit recipe is not as labor-intensive. Squid tubes are now available ready-cleaned, saving a lot of work. Squid, if not deep-fried in batter, is a good source of protein as well as Vitamins B_{12} and B_6, noted for preventing clogged arteries and heart disease.

> **OPTION**
> You can simply stuff the squid with 4 thawed Guisa Ice Cubes (page 17).

PREPARATION TIME 1 hour + 2 hours marinating time
YIELD 4 servings

4 large squid tubes, cleaned and thoroughly dried with paper towels
2 tablespoons annatto oil (page 50)

STUFFING
1 red onion, chopped
3 tablespoons + 1 teaspoon cane vinegar or sherry vinegar
1 small garlic clove, minced
4 tomatoes, diced
2 scallions, chopped
1 lime, zested and juiced
½ bunch cilantro, chopped
5 oz (150 g) kesong puti (white cheese), pressed or low-fat cream cheese
2 large green chilies, chopped
1 teaspoon fish sauce
1 teaspoon peppercorns, freshly cracked with a pestle

EQUIPMENT
4 bamboo skewers, cut 3 inches (7 cm) long from the pointed tip.

PER SERVING CALORIES 290KCAL FATS 14.12G | SATURATED FAT 3.9G PROTEIN 22.75G | CARBOHYDRATES 18.36G | FIBER 2.8G SODIUM 308MG | SUGARS 8.12G

1 Marinate the squid in the annatto oil for at least 2 hours. Make sure the squid is thoroughly dry for the oil to adhere to it.
2 Macerate the onion with the vinegar in a blender. Put in a bowl with all the remaining stuffing ingredients. Mix then strain. Set aside the strained stuffing.
3 Drain excess oil from the squid. Use some of it to grease the griddle.
4 Fill the squid tubes with the stuffing and fasten the opening with a skewer.
5 Heat a griddle over high heat. Sear the squid on each side for 30 seconds or until slightly charred. Lower the heat to medium and cook for 8–10 minutes on one side or until browned. If grilled too fast over high heat, the squid could burn before the stuffing cooks, or it could shrink and burst. Flip the squid over and cook for another 6 minutes.
6 Serve hot on top of black rice. Make 1-inch (2.5-cm) crosswise slits on the squid about 1 inch apart so that the cheese stuffing oozes over the rice.

Pinais na Pinaputok
Seabass, Vegetables and Rice Baked in Banana Leaf
by Jacqueline Chio-Lauri

PREPARATION TIME
30 minutes
YIELD 4 servings

¾ teaspoon sea salt
1 teaspoon garlic powder
1 teaspoon onion powder
1 teaspoon freshly ground pepper
4 sea bass fillets
2 Asian eggplants, roasted, see below
4 scallions, finely chopped
2-inch (5-cm) piece fresh ginger, grated
4 medium tomatoes, diced
A few sprigs thyme
4 banana leaves, each 12 inches (30 cm) long, washed and blanched, or equivalent size parchment paper or foil
2 cups (about 400 g) cooked rice blended with riced cauliflower
Olive oil, for drizzling

SAWSAWAN DIPPING SAUCE
4 calamansi, halved, or
   1 lemon, cut into wedges
1 teaspoon bagoong guisado shrimp paste (45 mg sodium/ teaspoon)

PER SERVING **CALORIES** 437KCAL
FATS 7.24G | **SATURATED FAT** 1.4G
PROTEIN 32.45G
CARBOHYDRATES 66.35G
FIBER 11.3G | **SODIUM** 608MG
SUGARS 13.52G

1 Preheat the oven to 450°F (230°C).
2 In a small bowl, mix the salt, garlic powder, onion powder and pepper to make a seasoning mixture. Season the fish with a pinch of the mixture. Set aside the rest.
3 Mash the eggplant with a fork. Sprinkle with a pinch of the seasoning mixture and stir.
4 In a bowl, combine the scallions, ginger, tomatoes, thyme and the remaining seasoning mix.
5 Place a quarter of the riced cauliflower mix about 3 inches (7 cm) from the edge of a banana leaf and spread to make a shape about the same size as the fish fillet. Top with a quarter of the mashed eggplant. Spoon about 1 tablespoon of the tomato mixture from Step 4 over the eggplant. Lay a fish fillet on top the mixture and cover with 2 more tablespoons of the tomato mixture. Drizzle with a few drops of olive oil. Fold the top and bottom edges of the leaf up and over and tuck the sides under the package or secure with cooking twine or the spine of the banana leaf. Repeat with the remaining fish.
6 Place the packages in a baking pan on the middle rack of the oven for 15 minutes. Open one and check if the fish is opaque. If not, rewrap and bake for another 2–3 minutes. Remove from the oven and let rest for a minute before serving.
7 To make the sawsawan dipping sauce, combine the calamansi juice with the bagoong. Open the fish packages and serve with the sawsawan on the side.

HOW TO ROAST WHOLE EGGPLANTS
Prick all sides of the eggplants with a fork or paring knife.
On an open flame: Cook directly on a gas stove over medium-high heat or over-the-fire grill turning it every 5 minutes until all the skin is charred and the eggplant is collapsed, tender and wrinkled.
In the oven: Preheat the oven broiler to maximum. Place pierced eggplants under the broiler on a baking tray lined with parchment paper or a silicone mat. Roast until they start to blacken, about 12–15 minutes depending on the eggplant size. Turn the eggplants over. Roast for another 10–15 minutes or until the eggplants are collapsed, completely tender and wrinkled. Slit the eggplants open and scrape the flesh out. Set aside and discard the skin.

MAKE-AHEAD TIP
Refrigerate uncooked packets for up to 3 days or cooked packets for up to 5 days. Reheat cooked packets individually in the microwave for 2–3 minutes.

This recipe combines elements of pinais (cooking in a pouch) and pinaputok (filling the cavity of a whole fish with stuffing).

CHAPTER 7

Karne
Meat

When Pigafetta, the chronicler of the Magellan-led Spanish expedition to the East Indies in 1519, was granted permission to set foot for the first time on the island of Mazaua, Raja Kolambu, the island's sovereign ruler ordered "a dish of pig's flesh" to be served. Although it was Good Friday, a day of fasting and abstinence from meat for Roman Catholics, Pigafetta didn't have the heart to say no. Sitting on a cane mat with legs curled up, they feasted on rice and pork from pigs that had been ritually slaughtered.

Sailing on to nearby islands, the scribe sighted goats, doves, tortoises, parrots and other exotic birds. Cows were later on introduced by the Spaniards and shipped in from Mexico. Despite the variety of meat protein sources in the Philippines, pork's popularity stood uncontested until 2019, when its per capita consumption was reportedly surpassed by chicken.

Recipes in this chapter are closely in line with the 2019 American Heart Health program, which recommends that a main dish should contain no more than 600 mg of sodium, 500 calories and 2 teaspoons of added sugars per serving.

Sharing Is Caring

Glen Ramaekers

Glen Ramaekers was born in the US to a Filipino mother and a Belgian father. He opened Humphrey, a Filipino-inspired restaurant in Brussels, whose menu is based around homegrown Asian vegetables and herbs from a family-owned garden run by Glen's wife, Julie and her father, Thierry de Block.

I've always considered myself athletic: I played basketball for eight years, mountain biked for eight years and practiced martial arts for twenty years. I led an active lifestyle, always on the go, seldom stopping to catch my breath. Up until 2018 — when way too often, agonizing pain started to pelt my neck and shoulder, spreading to my lower back, left hip and groin. These days, I can't even stand long enough to make myself a cup of coffee — let alone run a restaurant or keep up with my toddler's terrible twos.

Despite my condition, I can't afford to take a pause. It is a critical period. The partner who opened Humphrey with me in 2016 has left, leaving me to run the establishment by myself. The weight of meeting the expectations of guests, my staff and my family has fallen heavily on my back. Humphrey means more to me than a livelihood; it is who I am — it is my past, present and future.

At Humphrey, "sharing is caring" is our guiding principle, a philosophy that reflects Filipino culture. This is very visible in the region where my family is from — Negros, nicknamed Sugarlandia for its sugarcane plantation glory days. At festival time in Negros, like in most parts of the Philippines, folks open up their homes to welcome and feed everyone, including strangers. Villagers, even those deemed by Western standards as "not having much," share no less than everything they have. They go to great pains, spending days or weeks of preparation before the feast, so that they can offer everyone their best fare.

> *"At Humphrey, 'sharing is caring' is our guiding principle, a philosophy reflecting Filipino culture."*

> **"Who I am has been there all the time — knocking at the door, calling my attention, but drowned out by the demands of my busy existence."**

The restaurant's menu is also greatly influenced by the way of life of my grandmother and of two of my uncles, Tito Erning and Tito Roming. They lived in eco-sustainable stilt homes on a riverbank in Silay, nicknamed the "Paris of Negros," where pigs and cockerels roamed the ground beneath their bamboo-slatted floors. It's a taste of life I'd like to share with people at my restaurant, where the menu is led by homegrown and seasonal produce. During game season here in Belgium, for example, we've made dishes at my restaurant such as wild duck estopato sa tubo, a play on words I coined for estofado (a stew), pato (duck) and tubo (sugarcane). Game season is a nod to Sabong Sunday (cockfight Sunday) in Negros. On the Lord's day, menfolk gather around to engage in a popular sport called sabong, a practice that has existed since precolonial times, where roosters with sharp blades strapped to their spurs pit against each other until one of them flees or meets its end and winds up in someone's stew pot.

For over a year, even putting on a pair of trousers or any mundane chore that requires lifting my feet takes Herculean effort. I feel like Quasimodo weighed down by a virtual hump on my back as I limp through the restaurant's bright, open kitchen and mood-lit hardwood dining tables. But I plow on, emulating the carabao, a sickle-horned water buffalo regarded by many as the Philippines' national animal and a sugar plantation farmer's most valuable partner. Long after night has fallen, I return home to my wife and daughter, both already tucked in bed fast asleep.

Alas, even the most unwavering carabao loses it, too. If pushed too far beyond its limits, it's known to kick, ram and toss anything or anyone that crosses its path. Thus, before my pain does more harm than good to myself and everyone around me, I decide to seek treatment and take the doctor's advice to have an operation. Recovery will take from three to six months.

* * *

It's been three months since my surgery. My loved ones and I have been spending more waking moments together than ever before. Staying home has presented me with an opportunity to slow down, refocus and reflect. All along, I associated who I was with external things, searching high and low, crossing oceans to feel rooted, to establish a sense of connection. I don't know much, but in keeping with our belief of "sharing is caring," this I'd like to share with you. Who I am has been there all the time — knocking at the door, calling for my attention, but drowned out by the demands of my busy existence. No wonder I didn't find what I was looking for, because I was so preoccupied looking everywhere but deep within.

Estopato sa Tubo Duck Stewed with Sugarcane

Glen's recipe is reminiscent of a dish with Visayan origins called humba, a slow-cooked stew flavored with tausi (fermented black beans), common in Chinese kitchens. Duck humba is also called patotin in Ilonggo or pato tim nationally. Some versions of this dish cook the bird in naturally fermented coconut palm sap called tuba (coconut wine). Instead of muscovado or brown sugar, Glen sweetens the stew with unprocessed sugar cane. Duck has almost the same iron content as red meat, more than you get from chicken.

PREPARATION TIME 10 minutes
 + 2 hours stewing time
YIELD 2 servings

2 lbs (900 g) fresh or thawed frozen sugarcane,
  peeled and chopped
1 whole wild duck, halved, or 2 whole squabs;
  about 12 oz (350 g) total
6 cloves garlic, crushed
1 onion, quartered
1-inch (2.5-cm) piece ginger, crushed
2 star anise pods
3 tablespoons coconut aminos
½ cup (120 ml) coconut vinegar
1 tablespoon black pepper, crushed
¼ cup (50 g) Chinese fermented black beans
2½ cups (600 ml) water
1 small chayote or green papaya,
  peeled, deseeded and cubed
8 oz (250 g) long beans

1 Place all the ingredients, except the chayote and long beans, in a pot with 2½ cups (600 ml) of water. Cover the pot with a lid and bring to a boil over medium-high heat. Remove the lid and turn the heat to low. Cook, stirring and skimming off the fat once in a while, for about 1½ hours uncovered or until the leg joints feel loose when jiggled.

2 Put the chayote in the pan, on top of the duck. Turn the heat to medium high and let steam, covered, for 25 more minutes or until the chayote is almost tender. Add the long beans to the pot and cook for 10 more minutes or until tender and bright green. Transfer the vegetables to serving plates. Portion the duck and place on top of the vegetables. Drain and reserve the liquid from the pot and pour over the duck. Serve with your choice of grain.

PER SERVING CALORIES 510KCAL
FATS 27.9G | SATURATED FAT 8.7G | PROTEIN 35.32G
CARBOHYDRATES 29.1G | FIBER 7.1G
SODIUM 540MG | SUGARS 17.6G

The Meaning of Tinola

Rezel Kealoha

Rezel Kealoha is a food stylist and recipe developer with a focus on clean eating and healthy living. Her Instagram was chosen as one of the best to follow in 2018 by lifestyle blog The Identité Collective. She was a 2019 IACP (International Association of Culinary Professionals) Finalist for Best Editorial/Personal Food Photograph.

I lay in bed alone in a hospital room in Walnut Creek. The tears rolling down my face were not tears of joy. My arm, the port of entry for magnesium sulfate to trickle into my bloodstream, wasn't cradling my newborn baby. There were no murmurs of suppressed excitement from family and friends; no bouquets or balloons to liven up the room; no baby in sight. I fell in and out of sleep with scenes flashing in my head of how it should have been.

I was six years old when my aunt gave birth to her first child in the Philippines. Members of the family fussed over her; food of all kinds was brought in for her, conjuring up the image of the Three Kings bearing gifts for the Holy Nativity. While my aunt ate, her mother (my grandmother), who everyone called Nanay (Mother), tended to the newborn.

Tinola soup was on heavy rotation during the first three months after the birth. As soon as I heard Nanay hacking a whole chicken, I'd run into the kitchen. She chucked the chicken pieces into a huge pot and drizzled them with vegetable oil. Chunks of ginger and onions followed, and were stir-fried with the chicken to release their flavors. Before the bird browned, she let me pour the water into the pot until she said stop. She had a way of eyeballing how much of each ingredient should go into a dish.

When the soup was ready, Nanay would scoop some into a bowl and take it into my aunt's room with a plate of rice. She made sure that Auntie finished every morsel of it. The soup would help

> *"As soon as I heard Nanay hacking a whole chicken, I'd run into the kitchen. She chucked the chicken pieces into a huge pot and drizzled them with vegetable oil."*

> **"Mom arrived to stay with us at my request, she asked me what I wanted to eat. I answered, 'Tinola, please make me tinola.'"**

heal her body and give her the strength and nourishment to feed her baby.

My entry into motherhood couldn't have been further from this. Hours before I woke up in a hospital bed with a gauze pad taped across my abdomen, my husband and I were getting ready to watch the Super Bowl. Before the game started, I lumbered to the bathroom to preempt any urges to go during the game. There, in the bathroom, I thought I'd lost my thirty-week-old baby! My husband rushed me to the hospital.

Nurses hooked me up to machines and tested me nonstop for an hour or more. My blood pressure rose off the charts and my daughter's heartbeat slowed down. Major preeclampsia had struck out of the blue. The only way to save both myself and my daughter was for me to have a C-section. This meant my daughter would be born ten weeks premature.

When I regained consciousness after the C-section, I was wheeled into the Neonatal Intensive Care Unit (NICU). There she was, my daughter, in an incubator. Attached to it was a tag made by her NICU nurse. It read, "Happy Birthday Abby" followed by her weight, "2 pounds 15 oz [1.3 kg]." It took a while for the nurse to carefully extract Abby from the wires that were attached to her. When my newborn was finally handed to me, she fit in the palm of my hand. The nurse nestled her in the crook of my neck. As I held her, I whispered, "I'm sorry this has happened. I promise you; I'll take care of you."

I stayed in the hospital for seven days. Abby stayed for two months. I told everyone not to visit. I didn't want their first memory of her to be that of her miniature body covered in wires and tubes in an incubator. When Abby gained strength and was released from the hospital, I needed a week or two alone in the house with her before I asked my parents to come.

Finally, I could snuggle Abby into my arms without worrying about detaching any wires or breaking her. If she could feel my heart beating, I'm sure she could also feel it swelling with love. Her scent was intoxicating; I'd inhale it deeply. I swear it set off an overproduction of endorphins in my brain, for what else could explain the emotional high I felt? The pain, fear and the disappointment at what should have been receded to a distant past.

When Mom arrived to stay with us at my request, she asked me what I wanted to eat. I answered, "Tinola, please make me tinola."

Tinolang Manok
Chicken Ginger Soup with Cauliflower Mash

This American take on tinola uses spinach instead of malunggay (Moringa) leaves, which can be hard to find. The soup develops flavor in the oven over a few hours, leaving you free to do other things. Tinola is usually eaten with rice, but Rezel serves hers over a bed of mashed cauliflower.

PREPARATION TIME 2 hours
  + a few hours marinating time
  + 30 minutes resting time
YIELD 6 servings

TINOLA SOUP
¼ cup (60 ml) olive oil
¾ teaspoon coarse sea salt
1 tablespoon garlic powder
1 tablespoon onion powder
1 tablespoon black pepper, freshly ground
1 whole chicken, about 2½ lb 8 (1.1 kg), giblets removed
2-inch (5-cm) piece fresh ginger, peeled and cut into strips
1 onion, sliced
8 cups (about 2L) water
4 cups (120 g) baby spinach
8 oz (250 g) bok choy, cut into quarters

CAULIFLOWER MASH
1 lb (500 g) cauliflower, cut into florets.
1 tablespoon olive oil
¼ cup (60 ml) tinola broth
¼ teaspoon coarse salt
½ teaspoon pepper, freshly ground

PER SERVING CALORIES 548KCAL
FATS 40.2G | SATURATED FAT 9.2G
PROTEIN 38.3G | CARBOHYDRATES 8.6G
FIBER 3G SODIUM 592MG | SUGARS 2.2G

OPTION
Swap salt, garlic powder, onion powder and pepper for 3½ tablespoons Pinoy Powder (page 15).

1 Preheat the oven to 350°F (175°C).
2 Mix the oil, salt, garlic powder, onion powder and pepper in a bowl. Rub the inside and outside of the chicken with the mixture. Stuff half of the ginger and onion inside the chicken cavity. Cover the stuffed chicken and leave in the fridge overnight or at least for a few hours before cooking. Lay the bird breast down in a Dutch oven. Pour in 8 cups of water (the chicken will be partially submerged) and scatter in the rest of the ginger and onion. Cover with a lid and bake for 1 hour.
3 Remove the lid and bake for a further 30–45 minutes until the top of the chicken is golden brown and the broth starts to look a little oily from the rendered chicken fat. Take out of the oven and leave to rest for 30 minutes.
4 While the chicken rests, cook the cauliflower in a steamer or heat for 10 minutes until soft. Transfer to a bowl and mash. Add the oil and tinola broth a little at a time until you have the desired consistency. Season with salt and pepper.
5 Before serving, add the spinach and bok choy to the chicken broth and let wilt. Put some cauliflower mash in a bowl and ladle broth on top. Serve with a portion of chicken and spinach and bok choy on the side.

A Very Important Ingredient

AC Boral

AC Boral is the chef and owner of Asian-American restaurant and snack shop, Baba's House Kitchen in Oakland, California. Since 2014, AC has shared his unique take on Filipino identity with a brunch pop-up called Rice & Shine.

"A gravitational force stronger than myself pulled me toward the most unpopular among the spread of dishes. I went for laing ..."

My car crashed on the way home in the wee hours of the morning. I was in my mid-twenties. Fortunately, I walked away relatively unscathed. The car, however, didn't fare as well and needed to be scrapped. We were having lunch at my Uncle Dan's house that day and although I had every reason to stay home, I showed up at the party.

Bruised and still in something of a daze, I didn't understand what had gotten into me; maybe PTSD had kicked in or maybe my escape from death had compelled me to examine myself. Whatever it was, for the first time, instead of making a beeline for my usual favorite party fare, a gravitational force stronger than myself pulled me toward the least touched among the spread of dishes. I went for laing, a dish of taro leaves stewed in coconut milk with a color called "opaque couché," a sugar-coated term for a murky-looking greenish brown, voted as the world's ugliest color. I ladled some of it onto my plate. It wasn't exactly pleasing to the eye, but hey, looks could be deceiving.

Before that day, my earliest encounter with laing was vague or barely there. Uncle Dan had made it for a family party once. It looked sullen sat in a casserole dish like a wallflower.

Like most people, I had never given laing a second glance. Can you blame me? Next to the grandiose lechon (roasted pig), the king of Filipino family party foods, who would? Lechon always sat unchallenged, with batons of lumpia and heaps of pancit as its co-stars. Then, cast as extras were salads and vegetable dishes, like

> **"[Laing] evokes a powerful sense of time and place and has informed my journey as a chef. Even my vegan version [...] pleases palates and transports diners to their childhood."**

laing. They earned their place on the table maybe for the sake of diversity or maybe for the auntie who was trying to follow a diet.

Tasting laing for the first time was an experience. The fire of the chilies, the zing of the ginger, the sweetness of the coconut milk and the funk of the bagoong guisado shrimp paste set off a gustatory orgy. I knew laing was our ancestral Filipino dish. However, my dad, who was our immediate family's de facto chef, couldn't eat spicy food, so dishes like laing — specialties from our roots in Bicol — rarely graced our dinner table. The flavors connected me to a part of myself I had never had a chance to access. A part of me I needed to know.

Unusually quiet, I plopped myself down in a green plastic chair, intrigued by the laing I was eating. It sparked a different kind of hunger in me — a hunger to explore my culinary roots. This encounter would lead to a learning spree, not only about the dish and how it's prepared, but also about the wealth of gastronomic delights from the Bicol region that I had not known existed. I'd learn about the region's coconut-rich sweets, like linubak or nilupak, a chunky pudding made of banana, cassava or taro. I'd learn how anghang (chili heat) is a way of life.

Although this encounter with laing happened relatively late in life, the dish evokes a powerful sense of time and place and has informed my journey as a chef. Even my vegan version of the unassuming dish pleases palates and transports diners to their childhood. One of the most humbling compliments I've ever received is,

"This dish reminds me of my lola [grandmother]." Funny because my lola never made that dish for me and I had never eaten it in my childhood. It validates my claim to a dish and style of cooking I'm so new to, probably because I make it with a very important ingredient — honor for my ancestors and my roots.

Laing Pork and Taro Leaves in Coconut Milk

Laing or ginataang dahon ng gabi is also known as pinangat in the region of Bicol in southern Luzon, where taro leaves and coconut trees abound. Nowhere else in the country is food spiked as much with chilies (rich in vitamin C and antioxidants) as in Bicol, a practice which may have started out of necessity, to stretch dishes. Taro leaves are high in fiber and low in calories, so eating laing regularly is an excellent way to boost heart health and promote overall well-being.

PREPARATION TIME 45 minutes + 1 hour to season the pork + 8 hours to soak the taro leaves
YIELD 6 servings

1 teaspoon sea salt, divided
1 lb (500 g) pork shoulder, fat trimmed, diced small
2 tablespoons vegetable oil
4 cloves garlic, chopped
2 tablespoons ginger, minced
2 Thai chilies (more or less depending on taste), chopped
2 oz (60 g) dried shredded taro leaves, soaked for 8 hours and drained (reserving the soaking water), or 8 cups (560 g) fresh kale, packed and chopped, or a combination of both
4 cups (960 ml) light coconut milk
6 oz (200 g) fresh shiitake or chestnut mushrooms, sliced

1 Season the pork with ¼ teaspoon of salt. Leave in the fridge for at least an hour then drain.
2 Heat the oil in a pan over high heat. Add the pork and stir-fry until browned. Lower the heat to medium high. Add the garlic, ginger and chilies. Stir until the garlic turns golden.
3 Add the taro or kale leaves and the coconut milk. Cover and simmer for 1 hour, stirring occasionally. If it dries up, add some of water used to soak the taro leaves (or just water, if using kale).
4 Add the mushrooms and the remaining salt. Allow to simmer covered until most of the liquid has reduced, about 30 minutes.

PER SERVING CALORIES 400KCAL
FATS 26G | SATURATED FAT 7.3G
PROTEIN 18.6G
CARBOHYDRATES 26.3G | FIBER 4.5G
SODIUM 568MG | SUGARS 1.8G

The Joy of Meal Prepping

Jennifer Estacio

Los Angeles–based Jennifer Estacio is a mom of two kids. While working full-time in the marketing industry, she started a small business called Flipp Family to create a community for families to learn about Filipino culture through food and fun activities.

Drumming my fingers on my desk, I glance at the time display on my screen for the umpteenth time, willing it to advance to 4:30 p.m. I can't wait to rush to my second full-time job: motherhood. Looking at the photo next to my computer of my barely one-year old baby girl, Piper and two-year-old boy, Paxton, I wonder what developmental milestones they've crossed today while they were under the care of other people. I imagine my Paxton, throwing a ball overhand for the first time and my regret not being there to applaud his accomplishment. I imagine my Piper taking her first ever solo steps without my outstretched arms ready to catch her when she falls

As soon as the numbers 4:30 show on the screen, I race to my car to beat the rush hour traffic. I have to be on time to collect Paxton from daycare. During the hour or so drive, a gazillion questions run through my head: do I cook something different for dinner for my picky-eater son? What's in the fridge that we can reheat? Or maybe, should I pick up something to eat on the way home? What will the kids want to do after dinner?

"Mommy is here! That's my mommy!" cries out my boy upon seeing me. His excitement melts my heart. For a moment, all the stress of the day fizzles away.

Back in the car, my mind overwhelms me again with a long list of things to do. So much so that when we drive by Del Taco, In-N-Out and Chick-fil-A, the temptation to pick up a takeout dinner

> *"Do I cook something different for my picky-eater son? What's in the fridge that we can reheat? Or maybe, should I pick up food on the way home? What will the kids want to do after dinner?"*

> **"What is meal prepping? [...] It is the practice of planning, shopping and cooking all meals for the week on the weekends. Instead of spending an hour or so preparing meals every day you can prepare all meals for the week in just a few hours."**

grows stronger. But motherhood martyrdom wins the day. I take it as my duty to cook and feed my family healthy food as much as I can.

At home, I start whipping up a pasta dish for the little ones and preparing chicken, veggies and brown rice for me and my husband Lloyd. While I busy myself in the kitchen, a duet of screams and cries from hungry kids echoes in the background.

"Mommy, play with me! Let's go play!" calls Paxton.

That's my cue. It means chop chop, serve dinner NOW before all hell breaks loose!

"Pax, hold on, I'm getting dinner ready. Do you want to eat a snack so I can finish?"

"Mommy, I want to show you something!"

"OK, show Daddy!"

"No, only you, Mommy!"

My husband, Lloyd, jumps in and distracts him. I finish cooking their dinner first so they can eat while I make the rest. Piper can't sit still. Paxton runs back and forth from the table to the couch. I'm exhausted. Burnt out. I ask myself, why do I bother cooking every night?

By nine-thirty when the kids have gone to bed, Lloyd and I collapse on the sofa, too tired to talk to each other. While watching Netflix, I make a mental note to myself to restart a habit I had before becoming a mom — meal prepping.

What is meal prepping? Well, if you ever wonder how busy folks manage to stick to eating healthy meals every single day without the help of a personal chef, meal prepping is most probably the answer. It is the practice of planning, shopping and cooking all meals for the week on

the weekends. Instead of spending an hour or so preparing meals every day, you can prepare all meals for the week in just a few hours.

Filipino pork barbecue is one of my favorites. It lends itself well to meal prepping and everyone in the family likes it, too. Once cooked, it keeps in the fridge for three to five days. Stored in a container with side veg and rice, it makes a great packed lunch too, so it's pretty much grab and go in the morning.

* * *

Driving home from work and Paxton's daycare the following Monday, I feel lighter and unencumbered. My mind seems clearer and instead of the nonstop thread of questions that stream through my head while driving, I'm actually enjoying the ride. I make brief eye contact with Paxton through the rearview mirror and throw him a smile. Driving past the line of fast-food restaurants, I don't have to battle with feelings of guilty temptation. I know what we're having for dinner and most wonderfully, I know I don't have to cook.

When we arrive home, Paxton lines his toy cars on the floor. I sit on the floor next to him and push a car alongside his. I don't hear any screaming or crying that evening. Instead, I hear the vroom vroom sounds he makes at play, interspersed with squeals of glee.

Inihaw Pork and Vegetable Barbecue

This Filipino pork barbecue perfectly embodies the intermingling of tastes Filipinos love — it is at once sweet and subtly bitter (from the caramelization), aromatically spiced, tart and zesty, and packed with umami. The secret is in the marination. Cutting the pork in small thin strips gives more surface area to soak up the tasty marinade, avoiding the need to overseason. Using homemade banana ketchup and coconut aminos also allows us to cut down on sodium and sugar without sacrificing sarap (scrumptiousness).

PREPARATION TIME 30 minutes + at least 3 hours marinating/soaking time
YIELD 24 skewers or around 8 servings

1 cup Banana Ketchup (page 42)
¼ cup (60 ml) coconut aminos
3 cloves garlic, peeled and minced
3 tablespoons calamansi or lime juice
½ teaspoon ground pepper, divided
3 tablespoons sunflower oil, divided
4 lbs (1.8 kg) pork shoulder (fat trimmed) or loin, cut into thin 1-inch (2.5-cm) squares
2 red bell peppers, halved then quartered lengthwise to make 8 pieces
2 orange bell peppers, halved then quartered lengthwise to make 8 pieces
4 small zucchini, halved crosswise, then quartered lengthwise to make 8 pieces
Pinch of salt
24 bamboo skewers, soaked in water for about an hour if using a charcoal grill

1 In a bowl, mix the Banana Ketchup, coconut aminos, garlic, calamansi, half of the pepper and half a tablespoon of the oil until well combined.
2 Add the pork to the bowl. Mix until all the pieces of meat are coated with the marinade. Cover the bowl with plastic wrap. Store in the fridge and allow to marinate overnight or for at least 3 hours.
3 In a bowl, toss the zucchini and bell peppers with 2 tablespoons of the oil. Sprinkle with the remaining pepper and a pinch of salt. Mix well.
4 Thread the pork onto bamboo skewers. If using a stovetop griddle, make sure to cut the sticks to fit.
5 If using a griddle, brush it with oil on medium-high heat. Grill the skewers and vegetables for 5–7 minutes on each side until char marks are visible and the meat is cooked through.
6 Enjoy with a side of brown rice and Atchara Beetroot Relish (page 90).

PER SERVING CALORIES 406KCAL
FATS 18.4G | SATURATED FAT 5.1G
PROTEIN 43.7G
CARBOHYDRATES 14.8G | FIBER 0.8G
SODIUM 330MG | SUGARS 8.6G

Adobong Lechon Manok
Roast Chicken Adobo
adapted by Jacqueline Chio-Lauri

This is adapted from a recipe contributed by Luisa Brimble, lifestyle and food content producer and 2019 James Beard Award nominee for photography. A pairing of two popular Filipino cooking methods, adobo and lechon, this is not just a palate-pleaser, it's also easy to prepare. Lechon manok (roast chicken) mania first swept the Philippines by storm in the mid-80s when vendors of spit-roasted chicken appeared on almost every city street. Adobo sauce, instead of the sweet and sour chicken-liver sauce that is usually served with the Philippine rotisserie chicken, complements this tasty and heart-healthy favorite.

PREPARATION TIME 10 minutes
   + 60 minutes roasting time
YIELD 4 servings

1 garlic bulb, halved horizontally
   with the skin on
1 onion, quartered
3 bay leaves
3 garlic cloves, crushed to a paste
1 tablespoon Pinoy Powder (page
   15)
2 teaspoons freshly ground black
   pepper, divided
1 teaspoon olive oil
1 whole chicken, about 2½ lbs
   (1.1 kg)
2 stalks lemongrass, trimmed and
   bashed with a pestle or rolling pin
½ cup (120 ml) cane vinegar
1 tablespoon Pinoy Powder (page
   15) dissolved in 2 cups (480 ml)
   hot water
2 tablespoons coconut aminos
1½ lbs (750 g) green beans,
   blanched
⅓ cup (50 g) cashew nuts, pan-
   toasted without oil and salt

1 Preheat your oven to 360°F (180°C) or 320°F (160°C) if using a convection oven.
2 Spread out the garlic bulb halves, onion and bay leaves in a roasting pan or dish.
3 Mix the crushed garlic, 1 tablespoon Pinoy Powder, 1 teaspoon pepper and the oil in a small bowl. Rub the mixture all over the chicken. Stuff the lemongrass in the chicken cavity. Place the chicken in the roasting pan, breast side up, nestled on top of the aromatics.
4 Mix the vinegar, Pinoy Powder mixture and coconut aminos in a jug. Pour into the roasting pan around the chicken (not over it). This will become the adobo gravy.
5 Roast the chicken for 30 minutes or until nicely browned on top. The turn and roast for 30 minutes more. Insert a knife or skewer into the thickest part of the leg to check if it is cooked: if it is still a little pink, cook for 5–10 minutes more and check again.
6 Remove the chicken from the oven and rest for 5 minutes. Discard the bay leaves, garlic skin and lemongrass. Chop and divide into 4 portions.
7 In a bowl, toss the green beans and cashew nuts with about a third of the chicken adobo sauce. Divide into 4 servings, topped with the chicken and drizzled with adobo gravy. Serve with your choice of grain.

PER SERVING **CALORIES** 540KCAL
FATS 14.7G | **SATURATED FAT** 8.5G | **PROTEIN** 65G
CARBOHYDRATES 27.7G | **FIBER** 6.5G
SODIUM 585MG | **SUGARS** 9.13G

CHAPTER 8
Panghimagas
Sweets

The word "himagas" originally referred to the habit of eating fresh fruit or something sweet on the side to rid the palate of undesirable aftertastes. Now, it connotes dessert. Native sweets lean more towards fruits and kakanin, a native cake or pudding, whose name comes from the word "kanin" meaning cooked rice. Rice grains or milled rice and coconut milk are its main ingredients. The term kakanin also encompasses all kinds of native treats including cakes made from cassava.

Another type of panghimagas are frozen delights, like ice candy and sorbetes (more similar to sherbet than sorbet), a godsend in the Philippine's hot climate. Filipino ice candies are homemade stickless popsicles frozen in long plastic tubes. Sorbetes, on the other hand, is disparagingly called "dirty ice cream," perhaps due to its unregulated production and the fact that it's peddled on the streets. A sorbetero (ice cream vendor) pushing a brightly decorated cart housing canisters of sorbetes swaddled in salted shaved ice is an iconic fixture on the Philippine street food scene. The sorbetes is served scooped on a cone or in a bread bun.

Recipes in this chapter are closely in line with the 2019 American Heart Health program, which recommends that desserts should contain no more than 240 mg of sodium, 200 calories and 2 teaspoons of added sugars per serving.

For Love's Sake

Minerva Manaloto-Lott

Minerva Manaloto-Lott, aka Bebs, with her husband Armin Lott, created the popular Foxy Folksy, a personal Filipino food blog. Some of her works have appeared in Expo World Recipes, Chowhound, BuzzFeed, Well+Good, Homedit, Brit + Co and many other food-related sites, magazines and cookbooks.

"I landed at Frankfurt airport after what seemed like the longest and loneliest flight ever. And then a familiar face emerged."

The year 2012 was a time in my life defined by the things I had to give up and the things I learned anew. I'd just met Armin. He was as witty and charming as he was dorky and kind. I fell head over heels. Five months into our relationship, he proposed and I said yes. Looking back now, it did seem too fast.

When I met Armin he was living in Germany and I was in the Philippines. He came to the Philippines to see me four times that year — time couldn't fly quickly enough until we were together. By December, we had tied the knot. Armin returned to Germany after the wedding and I was to follow.

My final months in the Philippines swept by in a blur. I quit a promising job as a financial analyst at a good company. I bade colleagues and friends goodbye. And most difficult of all, I parted with my mama, papa and siblings, who were my world and my life.

Boarding the first leg of the flight alone, I managed to force a smile as flight attendants greeted me and pointed the way toward my seat. I walked down the aisle and slipped into my spot dry eyed. It was only when I pulled the seatbelt around my waist and the buckle clicked, that it hit me — I wasn't leaving for a vacation; I was leaving for good!

I wept silently the entire nineteen hours of my flight; it was a miracle I didn't faint from dehydration! A one-hour layover in Dubai was a slight distraction. But as soon as we took off again, I was back to crying my eyes out.

> **"Something was missing. Cooking Filipino dishes became my outlet to fill that void. Living far from the motherland not only made me crave for our food, but also gave me a deeper appreciation of our own cuisine."**

I landed at Frankfurt airport after what seemed like the longest and loneliest flight ever. And then a familiar face emerged. A smiling Armin greeted me as I entered the arrivals hall. His reassuring embrace abated the first pangs of misery and homesickness and reminded me of all the reasons why I'd decided to move across the globe.

In Germany, I was nothing like the independent, corporate ladder–climbing career woman I used to be. I was more like a toddler taking her first wobbly steps. I had to depend on Armin for every single thing. Not only did he gain a wife, he was also burdened with a child.

I learned some basic German before I left the Philippines but it was barely enough to get by on my own. Armin helped me every step of the way, translating for me, driving me any place I had to go and was always ready to catch me if I fell. He showed me the ropes: how to use public transport, enroll for German lessons and go shopping, the latter of which he was not a fan of. He supported my hobby, encouraging me to go public with my personal food blog. He bought me my camera equipment and books of food photography, and cheered me on all the way.

After some time, I found myself adapting to my new life. I got a job, made new friends from my German class and met several other Filipinas who took me under their wing. We gathered regularly and I'd bring kakanin cakes to fix everyone's cravings.

Everything was falling into place and I was finally fitting into my new home. But many times, at night, when Armin was fast asleep, I cried. I still yearned for my real home. Something was missing. Cooking Filipino dishes became my outlet to fill that void. Living far from the motherland not only made me crave our food, but also gave me a deeper appreciation of our own cuisine.

Over time, my blog grew beyond my expectations. I decided to quit my day job and work on it full-time. Armin floated the idea of moving to the Philippines. In late 2017, Armin quit his job too. We sold our belongings and booked our flights — one way. The Philippines is now Armin's home, as it is mine. Ah, the crazy stuff we do for love!

Pichi-Pichi, Espasol and Tibok-Tibok
A Trio of Filipino Cakes

This treat brings together a taste of three native kakanin cakes originating from three different provinces of the Philippines: pichi-pichi, a cassava cake from Quezon; espasol, a sweet made from galapong (glutinous rice flour) from Laguna; and tibok-tibok, a milk pudding from Pampanga. These sweets can last for up to 2–3 days at room temperature.

PREPARATION TIME FOR THE TRIO 40 minutes +
  30 minutes steaming time
YIELD 12 servings

Pichi-Pichi
Steamed Cassava Cakes Rolled in Coconut

Take care to cook the cassava thoroughly: it should never be eaten raw because of its cyanide content.

4 dried pitted dates, chopped
1 cup (240 ml) water
1 cup (225 g) grated frozen cassava, thawed (do not squeeze out the liquid)
2½ tablespoons sugar
½ teaspoon lye water, or 1 teaspoon baking soda solution (*see below)
6 tablespoons desiccated coconut soaked in ½ cup (120 ml) water

1 Place the dates and the cup of water in a blender or food processor. Puree until smooth.
2 Combine the pureed dates, grated cassava, sugar, and lye water in a bowl. Mix thoroughly.
3 Scoop into 12 molds (e.g., silicone muffin molds), using about 1½ tablespoons of the mixture for each mold.
4 Place in a steamer and steam for about 30 minutes or until the mixture becomes completely translucent.
5 Cool down completely for about 10 minutes. Remove each cake from its mold and roll in desiccated coconut.

PER TRIO SERVING CALORIES 196KCAL | FATS 8.4G
SATURATED FAT 5.9G | PROTEIN 1.8G | CARBOHYDRATES 29.6G
FIBER 1.2G | SODIUM 62MG | SUGARS 10.4G

* Dissolve ¼ tsp baking soda in 1 cup (240 ml) of water. Boil for 5 minutes. Let cool. Use 1 tsp for this recipe.

Espasol
Rice Logs Rolled in Toasted Rice Flour

¾ cup (100 g) glutinous rice flour
¼ cup (60 ml) coconut milk
2 tablespoons brown sugar
Pinch of salt
¼ cup (60 ml) water

1 Toast the flour in a skillet over low heat for 10–15 minutes, stirring occasionally until it turns slightly brown. Remove from the heat. Separate ¼ cup (35 g) of the rice flour and reserve to use in Step 4.
2 Combine the coconut milk, sugar and salt and ¼ cup water in a saucepan and bring to a soft boil while stirring occasionally to make sure the sugar dissolves.
3 Gradually add the toasted glutinous rice flour that has not been reserved, while stirring. The mixture will be very sticky so use a wooden spoon or other sturdy implement. Keep stirring until it forms into a sticky dough. It is ready when you turn a spoonful over and it holds its form.
4 Transfer the sticky dough to a flat surface that is generously dusted with the reserved toasted glutinous rice flour. Flatten the dough and shape into a rectangle about ½ inch (1 cm) thick.
5 Cut into 4 long logs using a knife or dough cutter. Then cut each log into 3 smaller pieces, making 12 pieces in total. Roll each piece in toasted rice flour to cover completely.

HOW TO TOAST DESICCATED COCONUT

Preheat the oven to 350°F (175°C). Line a baking sheet with a silicone baking mat or parchment paper. Spread the desiccated coconut on the lined sheet. Place in the oven for 3 minutes or until golden.

Tibok-Tibok

Milk Pudding

The name is an onomatopoeia for heartbeats, taken from the bubbling sound the pudding makes when it's cooking. Cashew milk replaces the richer and creamier whole carabao's milk, the original type of milk used for this pudding.

1 cup (240 ml) coconut milk
3 tablespoons granulated white sugar
Pinch of salt
¼ cup (30 g) cornstarch
1 cup (240 ml) cashew milk, divided
⅓ cup toasted desiccated coconut (see tip, above)

Make the latik (browned coconut milk curd)

1 Place the coconut milk in a skillet and bring to simmer over medium heat. Cook until the liquid has evaporated, leaving the solids (curd) and coconut oil. Stir from time to time to brown evenly.

2 Remove from the heat once the curd becomes light brown. It will continue to cook and brown while it cools down, so it should be removed from the heat before it burns. Strain the curd from the oil and set aside with some of the oil.

Make the tibok-tibok

1 Brush a mini loaf pan or similar container with a few drops of the oil used to cook the curd.

2 Mix together the sugar, salt and cornstarch in a small bowl. Add ¼ cup (60 ml) of the cashew milk. Stir well until the sugar is dissolved and the texture is smooth.

3 Place the rest of the cashew milk in a saucepan over low heat. Add the mixture from Step 2 into the pan through a sieve, to filter out any lumps. Let the pudding cook while stirring continuously with a wire whisk until it thickens and the first bubbles appear, about 10 minutes.

4 Immediately transfer the pudding to the mini loaf pan and give it a big tap to release trapped air and level out the pudding. Leave at room temperature until it cools down and sets. When set, cut into 12 squares. Top each piece with a pinch of curd and some toasted desiccated coconut.

5 Arrange a portion of each of these three cakes on a small dessert plate and serve.

Seal of Approval

Evan Cruz

Evan Cruz has held executive-chef level positions at various prominent restaurants and has worked as Chef, Director of Food and Beverage, and Area Executive Chef for the San Diego Marriott hotel group. He's now Corporate Executive Chef for the Cohn Restaurant Group in California and Hawaii.

> *"I hold a flurry of food memories from my childhood — hardly surprising because Nanay Chayong cooked all day every day!"*

A two-hour drive along an expressway north of Manila takes you past verdant rice paddies, lush banana plantations and thatched-roof nipa huts. It leads to a place where sprawling craggy peaks and valleys meet a sickle-shaped coastline. It is the land of my birth. It is Olongapo.

For most of the twentieth century, until 1992, Olongapo was also home to a major United States Navy facility. Dad served in the Navy, which paved my mother's path to the US. I was only three years old when my mother migrated. She left me in the care of my paternal and maternal grandmothers, whom I both call Nanay (Mother). I stayed with them for seven months before I joined my mother in the US.

Some years later, my nanays would also move to the US. Because Dad was always away at sea and Mom always at the hospital where she worked as a nurse, my nanays were the ones who practically raised me.

I hold a flurry of food memories from my childhood — hardly surprising because Nanay Chayong cooked all day every day! I remember distinctly the smell of dilis (dried anchovies) greeting me in the morning. Nanay stir-fried them with the perfect blend of sugar and fresh chilies creating an umami aroma that was similar to aged cheese.

Close to midday, I'd hear Nanay's pestle knocking against the mortar. She'd be crushing garlic for pancit. I was too little to see into the vast stovetop kawali (wok), but I remember watching her toss a huge mound of white,

> **"Cooking didn't figure on the success score card! So, no one leapt with glee when I became a chef, not even Nanay. Talk about hard to please!"**

fluffy bihon rice noodles into it. After lunch, but before the meal had had time to settle down in our bellies, she'd be back in the kitchen again preparing merienda (snacks). Turon, a sugar-glazed lumpia roll stuffed with saba banana, was one that she often made.

Nanay Chayong gave her all when she cooked and expected the same from her protégé — me. By the time I was eleven years old, my culinary abilities had grown. As well as helping her fry chicken, peel snow peas, shave carrots and string long beans, I also learned how to cook rice. We didn't use a rice cooker, so this was my biggest hurdle. She taught me never to throw the rice water away. It had to be reserved for thickening sinigang soup. If I burnt the rice pot once, I'd get a scolding. If I burnt it once more, I'd get the tsinelas (slipper)! Once, I overwatered the rice to avoid burning the pot. The rice turned too sludgy to eat. To rescue me from getting punished, my grandpa used the rice to glue together sheets of old newspaper and twigs from a walis ting-ting broom to make a kite.

Lumpia rolling was another challenge. I did my best to try and master the technique of placing the filling on the wrapper evenly and rolling it tightly into a firm cylinder, but I rarely met Nanay's high standards. She might sneak up behind me and correct me, or she would open up the rolls and redo them herself, or sometimes she'd make me do them all over again. When she'd had enough of my efforts, she'd exile me out to play.

With all the cooking that went on, you'd think that my family would have seen it coming — that I'd wind up being a chef. Unfortunately not! They had "higher" hopes for me. Being the eldest son and the eldest grandson of the family, the measure of my family's success lay in my hands, particularly, in what I did for a living. Cooking didn't figure on the success score card! So, no one leapt with glee when I became a chef, not even Nanay. Talk about hard to please!

It wasn't until a few years ago that I had a breakthrough. A food writer friend of mine wanted to learn more about Filipino food. I brought her to meet Nanay Chayong. Nanay was eighty-three years old by then. She walked with the aid of a cane and did most tasks sitting down. She showed my friend how to make turon. She rolled the saba banana into a wrapper perfectly as she always did when she rolled lumpia. I rolled a few myself, too and waited for Nanay's reaction. Silence. After strict scrutiny, all made it into the fryer. Victory! I had passed her seal of approval.

Turon aka Lumpiang Saging Banana Rolls

Turon is technically not a kakanin cake, but this take on the banana spring roll uses glutinous rice flour for its wrapper, creating a connection with the native sweet. The type of banana used for turon is called saba, also known as sweet plantain. Turon, like its "naked" relative, bananacue (caramelized saba banana on a stick), is sold on the streets in many towns and cities in the Philippines, especially outside schools at recess and dismissal time. The traditional turon is made in the same way as lumpia: deep-fried and rolled in ready-made egg roll wrappers. Evan's turon recipe avoids the deep-frying, but delivers a crepe-like wrapper with a slight crunch.

PREPARATION TIME 45 minutes
YIELD 10 lumpia

FOR THE FILLING
1 tablespoon avocado oil
5 medium-sized saba banana
  or 3 plantains, sliced
3 tablespoons brown sugar
Pinch of sea salt

TURON WRAPPERS
1⅔ cups (200 g) all-purpose flour
½ cup + ½ tablespoon (90g) mochiko
  or glutinous rice flour
¼ teaspoon fine sea salt
2⅓ tablespoons sugar
1½ tablespoons avocado oil
  + a little for greasing pan
2½ cups (600 ml) water

PER SERVING CALORIES 194KCAL
FATS 4.08G | SATURATED FAT 0.7G
PROTEIN 3.49G
CARBOHYDRATES 50.39G | FIBER 2.4G
SODIUM 76MG | SUGARS 16.3G

Make the filling

1 Heat the oil in pan over medium heat until it shimmers. Add the sliced banana and spread all over the pan. Stir carefully. Add the sugar and stir to coat the banana. Allow to cook, stirring occasionally until the sugar caramelizes, about 5 minutes. Sprinkle with the salt.
2 Set the filling aside while making the turon wrappers.

Make the turon wrappers

1 Sift the flours, salt and sugar in a medium bowl and mix with a whisk. Add the oil and 2½ cups water and mix with a whisk or hand mixer until well blended and smooth. The batter should be as thick as heavy cream and thin enough to easily swirl and spread over the pan in Step 2.
2 Place a nonstick sauté pan over medium-high heat. Lightly brush the pan with little oil. Lift the pan off the heat, ladle about a quarter cup of batter into the pan, swirling it quickly for the batter to spread out. Place the pan back on the heat and spread the batter as thinly and evenly as possible using a crepe spreader or spatula. Cook until light brown, about 1–2 minutes. Flip the wrapper over and cook lightly. Keep warm in a preheated oven. Repeat until you have 10 wrappers.
3 Place about 2 tablespoons of the banana mixture across the lower third of a wrapper, about 1 inch (2.5 cm) from the bottom edge. Fold the lower side up over the filling and roll tightly leaving the sides open. Serve warm.

The Juice Fast

Francis Maling

Francis Maling has roots in Manila but grew up in Queens, New York. A graduate of The Culinary Institute of America, he's worked in many kitchens all over NYC from fine dining establishments to places selling street food. He hopes to share his take on Filipino food with his latest project, a pop-up called Bad for Business.

> *"I'd pushed myself to breaking point, ignoring distress signals from my body, including the pain radiating from my right shoulder."*

A sharp, stabbing pain shot through my chest. I was huffing and puffing as if I'd run up the eighty-six flights of stairs of the Empire State Building, when in reality, my legs had been stretched out on the sofa for hours while I watched Netflix. If I hadn't just passed the full battery of tests prescribed for me by my cardiologist, I'd be scrambling for my phone to hit 911.

My weight had always been an issue. When I was growing up in the Philippines, I was a chunky kid feasting frequently on barrels of Jollibee's Chickenjoy. But it was here in New York, in my early twenties, when my weight ballooned to a morbid 260 pounds [118 kg]. I could no longer blame the Chickenjoy, but my diet wasn't any better. In fact it was probably worse, not to mention the bottles of booze I guzzled to boot.

It wasn't just about the weight. Working in the restaurant industry is known to induce mental problems that can lead to substance abuse, alcoholism and depression — more so than almost any other career field. Everyone is always on edge and tempers flare up at the slightest infraction. I'd pushed myself to breaking point, ignoring distress signals from my body, including the pain radiating from my right shoulder.

One day, like most others, I had come to work barely having slept. Chronic anxiety was depriving me of many things, including much-needed slumber. As usual in the kitchen, tickets piled up, cooks yelled back and forth and wait staff carrying plates rushed around. A hamachi dish was called

> **"[...] my most extreme experience of vegetarianism had been eating pinakbet vegetable stew, loaded with bagoong guisado shrimp paste and generous slices of crispy deep-fried pork belly [...]. Yet I lasted the thirty days, not only without a morsel of meat, but also without any solid food."**

for pick up, awaiting ricotta from my station. Unfortunately, I f*cked it up; the ricotta didn't set correctly and ran like milk sludge. The head chef picked up my half-assed dish then slammed it back down on my workstation. His action triggered a panic attack. I felt faint. I gasped for air as if I was running out of oxygen.

To prevent a nervous breakdown, my mind learned to black out humiliating and traumatic incidents as a coping mechanism. But anxiety would still seep into my system even in the absence of a triggering incident — even if I was lying on my sofa binge-watching shows on Netflix.

At home, Isa, my girlfriend, who happens to be a nurse, helped me through my episodes. She'd sit by me, ask me to take a long, slow, deep inhale then exhale fully. "There's nothing wrong with your heart," she'd say in a soothing voice, "it's all in your mind."

But I did need to heal my body. Aside from the extra pounds I had amassed, I had to mend a tendon in my right shoulder torn from pressing weights at the gym. An orthopedic doctor had recommended surgery, a remedy I didn't want to take given the long post-operation recovery; it would mean a lot of time off work. To manage the pain, I was relying heavily on prescribed anti-inflammatory drugs, which were not a cure. I was at the end of my rope. It was time to try something else, something radical, something that could reboot my system and keep me from heading toward the grave. A documentary I saw on Netflix titled *Sick, Fat and Nearly Dead* offered

an option that could jump-start the body's ability to heal itself by juice fasting. Only fruit and vegetable juices for me — for thirty days!

Before then, my most extreme experience of vegetarianism had been eating pinakbet vegetable stew, loaded with bagoong guisado shrimp paste and generous slices of crispy deep-fried pork belly called bagnet. Yet I lasted the thirty days, not only without a morsel of meat, but also without any solid food.

* * *

I lost thirty pounds [14 kg]. The inflammation in my shoulder doesn't hurt as much and I've been able to wean myself off of my medication. I continue practicing breathing techniques. I run outdoors to exercise my body and clear my mind. If offered crispy pata (pork leg), lechon (roast pig) or the like, I'd say, "Of course!" But I make sure not to load my plate with it. There's a wealth of delectable items I'd like to leave room for in the well-balanced life I strive for. Ultimately, it's all about concocting the right blend — one that'll sustain me with a longer-lasting joy.

Ice Candy

Unlike commercial freeze pops, Filipino ice candy is made of fresh fruit juice poured into plastic tubes. It looks like a milkshake, but it's mixed with blended fruit, such as melon, avocado, young coconut, or pureed ube (purple yam) or even monggo (mung beans). These refreshing ices are like manna from heaven especially from March to May, the peak months of summer in the Philippines.

PREPARATION TIME 10 minutes
  + 3 hours or more freezing time
YIELD 1 quart (1 L) or 6 ice candies per flavor

EQUIPMENT
Reusable squeezy popsicle molds
Small pitcher or jar with a spout

BANANA ICE CANDY
1 large cucumber, peeled, cut into small cubes
1 large ripe banana, thinly sliced
2-inch (5-cm) piece fresh ginger, peeled,
  cut into thin slivers
1 green apple, peeled, cut into small cubes
½ lemon, juiced
3 cups (720 ml) oat milk
1–2 teaspoons honey, to taste, optional

WATERMELON AND PAPAYA ICE CANDY
⅓ cucumber, peeled, cut into small cubes
½ ripe papaya, cut into small cubes
2-inch (5-cm) piece fresh ginger, peeled,
  cut into thin slivers
2 cups (300 g) watermelon, seeded, small cubes
3 cups (720 ml) coconut water
1–2 teaspoons honey, to taste, optional

1 Place the ingredients for each flavor inside a blender. Blend on high for 1 minute until well combined.

2 Transfer the mixture into a pitcher or jar with a spout. Pour into popsicle molds with lids.

3 Place in the freezer for 3 hours or overnight until frozen.

BANANA ICE CANDY
PER SERVING
CALORIES 93KCAL
FATS 2.6G
SATURATED FAT 0.17G
PROTEIN 4.6G
CARBOHYDRATES 13.92G
FIBER 1.08G
SODIUM 58.3MG
SUGARS 11.21G

WATERMELON AND PAPAYA
ICE CANDY PER SERVING
CALORIES 46KCAL
FATS 0.4G
SATURATED FAT 0.25G
PROTEIN 1.34G
CARBOHYDRATES 10.16G
FIBER 1.83G
SODIUM 128.3MG
SUGARS 7.53G

Lolo's Medicine

Christiana Marie Cunanan

Christiana Marie Cunanan is the founder of Cheeri Cheeri, a handcrafted Filipino vegan ice cream pop-up. For the past eight years, she has worked full-time in production management at Walt Disney Animation Studios making her one of the few Pinays at the entire studio.

"Time with you is medicine."

My lolo (grandfather), Cesar, would take his time reciting this phrase every single moment he was around me or my younger sister, Cathy. As he firmly uttered the words, I could feel his focus and sweet smile on us like a lingering hug.

Even in his late seventies, he swore by that statement when it came to his family. "I stay young and my mind stays young because of you. You are my inspiration," he'd say. I heard that so often throughout my life that I wholeheartedly believed he was invincible, immortal even.

However, years would pass when I didn't see my grandparents. Not only was it an issue of time, but distance too. When I turned eight, my grandparents left Southern California to retire to the Philippines. FaceTime did not exist yet, which meant expensive international calls consisting of quick exchanges. I thought saying "I love you" was medicine enough for my "superman."

In 2011, after six years of separation, I flew to Pampanga in the Philippines to visit them. At the airport, I was greeted by their big smiles and long lingering hugs like before. The only difference was in the strength of their embrace; they seemed to have lost some muscle power. It was a subtle difference but it made a huge impact on me. I thought my lolo and lola must have missed us, their regular dose of "medicine."

Alarmed, I suddenly realized the value of choosing who to be with, when and where, of giving my attention and time to what truly matters.

> *"I suddenly realized the value of choosing who to be with, when and where, of giving my attention and time to what truly matters."*

> "As if crafting a medicine for myself and others,
> I chose to honor Lolo through the ice cream
> that I make, doing my best to infuse my recipes
> with his youthful 'eager to share' spirit."

I am thankful that after that eye-opening visit, I was lucky enough to visit them once or twice a year, sharing loving moments like we did when Cathy and I were little, until Lolo passed peacefully in 2017.

I miss my lolo dearly and try to build my connection with him into my life. One way of doing this is through my efforts to make his concept of "medicine" more accessible and palpable. As if crafting a medicine for myself and others, I chose to honor Lolo through the ice cream that I make, doing my best to infuse my recipes with his youthful "eager to share" spirit.

Particular flavors—like for me, ginataang bilo-bilo (sweet rice balls in coconut milk)—can connect us back to a time we shared with people we love. I hope to give that sliver of time back to all, where they can feel the "cheer" with those that have always mattered. My ice creams are delightfully simple, story-filled and special — all of which are values worth sharing.

Ginataang Langka Sorbetes
Jackfruit and Coconut Ice Cream

The flavor of this dairy-free ice cream is inspired by a sweet, warm treat called ginataang bilo-bilo with langka (rice balls and jackfruit cooked in coconut milk with sago pearls), a dish often made at home by lolos and lolas. Christiana omits the rice balls in this delicious frozen take on the ginataan, a dish that she enjoys sharing with her loved ones!

PREPARATION TIME 30 minutes
  + 3 hours freezing time
YIELD 4 servings

SORBETES
20-oz (600-g) can ripe jackfruit, drained
  + 1 tablespoon of the syrup
⅓ cup (80 ml) coconut milk
1 teaspoon olive oil

TOPPING
2 cups (480 ml) water
¼ cup (40 g) tapioca or sago pearls
½ cup (120 ml) coconut milk

Make the sorbetes

1 Place all the ingredients in a blender and blend thoroughly.
2 Pour the blended mixture into a freezer-safe container.
3 Freeze for 3–5 hours.
4 Scoop when ready to eat.

Make the topping

1 In a saucepan, bring the 2 cups of water to a boil. Pour the tapioca pearls into the pot. Cook for about 15 minutes or until the tapioca is translucent and chewy. Drain.
2 Garnish each scoop of ice cream with a sprinkling of tapioca. Drizzle each portion with 2 tablespoons of coconut milk.

PER SERVING CALORIES 199KCAL | FATS 11.23G
SATURATED FAT 10G | PROTEIN 1.13G | CARBOHYDRATES 25.85G
FIBER 0.5G | SODIUM 13MG | SUGARS 3.17G

Coffee with a Mission

Sam Magtanong

Beverly Magtanong is a professional opera singer, Jelynn Malone a Hollywood film and TV actor, Mike Arquines a traditionally trained chef and Sam Magtanong an infantry officer deployed to Iraq from 2005–2007. Together, they opened and run Mostra Coffee in San Diego, named 2020 Roaster of the Year by *Roast Magazine*.

"Her story captured both my heart and my imagination with all the possibilities and opportunities to give back and reconnect with my roots."

"Hey Sam! Jelynn and I are going to start a business," announced my wife, Beverly.

I looked at her with a puzzled expression. *Wow! She's a professionally trained opera singer and her best friend, Jelynn, is a Hollywood actress – what do they know about business?*

Wanting to humor my wife, I politely asked, "What kind of business are you thinking of starting?"

Beverly replied, "A specialty coffee roasting business!"

Wait a minute, what?

Unable to hold my tongue any longer, I blurted, "But, you don't even drink coffee!! What do you know about roasting coffee!"

The intensity in her voice was notable as she described their vision for the company and the purpose behind it.

Back in 2009, Beverly and Jelynn, who were childhood friends, had traveled to the Philippines to help build homes for local families with a charity group. They saw two sides of the Philippines – the beautiful culture and people, the gorgeous countryside and pristine beaches; and the flip side – the widespread and deep-rooted poverty. It made a big and lasting impact on them.

The two felt compelled to help. They spoke with nonprofits working in the area and figured that the best way to help out would be to create economic opportunities that could generate living-wage jobs and improve lives in the poorer areas of the Philippines.

It was a tall order for two women in their twenties at the time, and one they didn't

> "Starting this coffee company was about identity and purpose [...]. Building a respected coffee brand that could bring Philippine coffee to an international market was a personal mission."

immediately know how to tackle. Nonetheless, they had never given up the idea of starting a business that could help change lives, and they finally settled on coffee, one of the Philippines' agricultural products.

Once the bombshell of Beverly's announcement of starting a specialty coffee roasting business in San Diego sank in, her story captured both my heart and my imagination with all the possibilities and opportunities to give back and reconnect with my roots.

"Let's do it!" I said.

We pooled our savings to buy a coffee-roasting machine and our first bags of green coffee. We started the company in the garage. Since Beverly, Jelynn and myself didn't know anything about roasting coffee, we partnered with Mike Arquines, a friend who had the most knowledge in our group about coffee and the industry. With a history of working in Michelin-rated restaurants and running his own custom-dining experience, Mike took the lead in developing the company's coffee program, but even he was new to coffee roasting.

But Mike's creative ability and his sense of purpose blew us away; he had dropped out of an RN nursing program a semester away from graduation to pursue his passion in culinary arts. We trusted him as our company's head coffee roaster.

Mike suggested incorporating Filipino desserts into our coffee menu program as a way of highlighting our culture. Jelynn then remembered the most amazing dessert she had tasted for the first time when she visited the Philippines. Her tita (aunt), delighted at seeing her after so many years, made Buko Pandan for her. Jelynn raved about how delicious the young coconut salad was and about the love she felt in the room as her tita beamed with joy at this family reunion.

Inspired by the delicious Filipino dessert and of Jelynn's memory, Mike created the Buko Pandan Latte.

For all of us, a drink like this evokes memories of our families and home. I was born in the Philippines. For me, starting this coffee company was about identity and purpose. My grandfather was a rice farmer who toiled on the land for sixty years before he passed away. My mother, the eldest of fifteen children, was the only one who was able to come to America. Building a respected coffee brand that could bring Philippine coffee to an international market was a personal mission for me, as it was for Beverly, Jelynn and Mike.

Mostra's goal is to put Philippine coffee on the map. In 2019, *Roast Magazine* announced Mostra Coffee as the 2020 Micro Roaster of the Year, due in part to our work in supporting Philippine coffee farmers.

I remember in 2013 when we started the company in the garage. Beverly said, "I feel it in my heart. I know that if we follow our heart and our passion, we can't go wrong."

Buko Pandan Latte
Coconut and Pandan-Flavored Coffee

This recipe by Mike Arquines embodies the refined simplicity of buko pandan, a delicious Philippine dessert. Buko (young green coconut), with its well-documented health benefits, shines in this after-meal treat. It gives the beverage depth and complexity, while imbuing a sense of comfort. In concert with the flavor of pandan (fragrant screwpine), each sip of this coffee floods the Filipino palate with nostalgia.

PREPARATION TIME 2 minutes
YIELD 1 serving

Double shot of espresso, about ¼ cup
  (60 ml)
1 tablespoon Pandan Syrup (see
  facing page)
1 cup (240 ml) Buko Milk (see facing
  page)
Pinch of coconut sugar for dusting,
  optional

PER SERVING CALORIES 207KCAL
FATS 9.3G | SATURATED FAT 6.9G
PROTEIN 9.4G | CARBOHYDRATES 22.3G
FIBER 1.1G SODIUM 142MG | SUGARS 21.4G

1 Pull the espresso into a 12 oz (350 ml) cup. Add the Pandan Syrup.
2 Pour the Buko Milk into a stainless or heatproof jug. Steam and texturize the Buko Milk using the steam wand on an espresso machine. Alternatively, you can heat the milk on a stovetop then froth with a handheld milk frother. Make sure you don't scald the milk. The temperature should not exceed 180°F (82°C). Another alternative is to froth the milk using the method in the box below.
3 Pour the milk into the center of the cup containing the espresso and syrup. Give the cup a few gentle taps on the table to allow the denser foam to rise to the top.
4 Sprinkle a pinch of coconut sugar on top of the froth.

HOW TO FROTH MILK WITHOUT A FROTHER
Pour milk in a glass jar with a screw lid filling no more than a third of the jar. Close the jar with the lid and shake vigorously for a few seconds or until the milk has almost doubled in volume.

Remove the lid and warm in the microwave for 30 seconds. Watch to make sure it doesn't overflow. If it overflows, turn off the microwave and allow the foam to settle. Keep heating in 30-second increments until the milk is warm and frothy.

Buko Milk

PREPARATION TIME 2 minutes + 18 hours
YIELD Approximately 3 quarts (3 L)

1 lb (500 g) frozen shredded buko or
   young coconut
3 quarts (3 L) non-fat milk
1 vanilla bean pod, split and scraped
   or 1 tablespoon vanilla extract
4 cups (960 ml) water

1 Place all the ingredients in a food-safe
   container. Stir to thoroughly combine.
   Place in the fridge, covered, for 18 hours.
2 Stir and strain the mixture through a fine
   mesh strainer. Discard the pulp. Pour the
   milk into an airtight container and store
   in the fridge. Will keep for 5 days.

Pandan Syrup

PREPARATION TIME 10 minutes
YIELD Approximately 1 cup (240 ml)

1 cup (240 ml) coconut water
5 pieces pandan leaf, each about 1 inch (2.5 cm)
¼ cup (40 g) coconut sugar
½ vanilla bean pod, split and scraped
   or ½ tablespoon vanilla extract

1 Combine all the ingredients in a saucepan
   and bring to a boil. Boil for 5 minutes while
   stirring periodically. Ensure the sugar is
   dissolved completely.
2 Remove from the heat. Pour through a fine
   mesh strainer (squeezing out as much liquid
   from the pandan leaves as possible) and chill
   in an ice bath. Store in an airtight container in
   the fridge. Will keep for 3 weeks.

Acknowledgments

My heartiest thank you to:

• You, dear reader, knowing that you've read this book is what it's all about.

• The esteemed contributors, photographers, and supporters of this project, there is no telling what we can accomplish when we work together, especially if we put our hearts into it. You are the beating heart of this book. Own it!

• Rezel, you've done an incredible job in painting a thousand words in every picture.

• The officials at the Philippine Embassies/ Consulates and to everyone who has connected me with contributors, potential contributors, or collaborators for this project, I really appreciate it!

• Martha, my cookbook agent and to Melissa, Ellie, Rupy, Betty Ann, Lisa, Kyla, and Youssef, for the reviews.

• Doris, my bestie, you're a gem!

• My family specially to Ate Joy, for letting me bounce ideas off you, for playing devil's advocate, and for inspiring excellence. You and Kuya Jude are a force to be reckoned with; Mom & Dad, thanks for the prayers, sacrifice and unwavering vote of confidence; Diane, for being my link to a wealth of sources in the Philippines; And to my amori, Leo & Raff, my life muses, and my driving force for cooking healthy. I love you all.

• The Tuttle Publishing team especially Cathy who shepherded this book to the finish line.

• And most of all, thank you Lord for blessing my life with countless miracles, including the opportunity to be able to work on projects I deeply care about, such as this. To You be the glory!

Photo Credits

Rezel Kealoha: Pages 2–4, 15, 17, 27, 35, 36, 41, 43, 47, 51, 53, 61, 65, 68, 71, 73, 79, 83, 86, 89, 97, 101, 105, 109, 112, 115, 121, 124, 130, 133, 135, 140, 143, 146, 149, 151, 152, 161, 164, 167, 171.
Jacqueline Chio-Lauri: Pages 9, 88, 91.
Grace Guinto: Page 70.
Cynthia Cherish Malaran: Page 74.
Reyshiel Andres: Page 127.
Minerva Manaloto-Lott: Page 157.
Shutterstock: Background pattern: RedKoala. Page 5, left, sundaemorning; right, Al.geba. Page 6, left, Ivan Trizlic; right, Maria Maarbes. Page 7, top, Ron Frank; middle, yoshi 0511; bottom, Stuckmotion Patterns. Page 8, left, Yatra4289; middle, MDV Edwards; right, Adrian Baker. Page 10, left, vandycan; right, Alex Bogatyrev. Page 11, top left, Rifad; bottom left, anny ta; top right, Regreto. Page 12, left, julie deshaies; right, Boonchuay1970. Page 13, left, MR.ANUWAT; right, Andi WG. Page 16, top right, Loybuckz. Page 18, R.M. Nunez. Page 20, Dpongvit. Page 21, LungMan. Page 23, Lesterman. Page 24, instant pot, Doyel Design. Page 46, carrots, ChristosGeorghiou; mushrooms, andrey oleynik; peas, Sketch Master. Page 50, theorph. Pages 54, 92, junpinzon. Page 77, Oscar Espinosa. Page 90, Epine. Page 104, Mirt Alexander. Page 116, Dream Architect. Page 145, Dorothy Puray-Isidro.
Dreamstime: Page 16, top left, Johari Jamalluddin; Page 54, Bhofack2. Page 136, Bill Roque.

Writing Credits

All contributor essays were written by the contributor except for pages 25–26, 32–33, 48–49, 56–57, 62–63, 66–67, 69–70, 80–81, 84–85, 102–103, 106–107, 110–111, 113–114, 122–123, 138–139, 144–145, 147–148, 158–159 and 162–163, which were cowritten by Jacqueline Chio-Lauri. Pages 29–30 were written by Paige Liwanag.

Index of Main Ingredients

Published by Tuttle Publishing, an imprint of
Periplus Editions (HK) Ltd.

www.tuttlepublishing.com

Copyright © 2023 Jacqueline Chio-Lauri

Library of Congress Control Number: 2023937312
ISBN: 978-0-8048-5466-5

Distributed by
North America, Latin America & Europe
Tuttle Publishing
364 Innovation Drive
North Clarendon, VT 05759-9436, USA.
Tel: 1 (802) 773-8930
Fax: 1 (802) 773-6993
info@tuttlepublishing.com
www.tuttlepublishing.com

Japan
Tuttle Publishing
Yaekari Building 3rd Floor
5-4-12 Osaki
Shinagawa-ku
Tokyo 141-0032
Tel: (81) 3 5437-0171
Fax: (81) 3 5437-0755
sales@tuttle.co.jp
www.tuttle.co.jp

Asia Pacific
Berkeley Books Pte. Ltd.
3 Kallang Sector #04-01
Singapore 349278
Tel: (65) 6741 2178
Fax: (65) 6741 2179
inquiries@periplus.com.sg
www.tuttlepublishing.com

26 25 24 23
10 9 8 7 6 5 4 3 2 1

Printed in China
2307EP

TUTTLE PUBLISHING® is a registered trademark of Tuttle Publishing, a division of Periplus Editions (HK) Ltd.

"Books to Span the East and West"

Tuttle Publishing was founded in 1832 in the small New England town of Rutland, Vermont [USA]. Our core values remain as strong today as they were then — to publish best-in-class books which bring people together one page at a time. In 1948, we established a publishing outpost in Japan — and Tuttle is now a leader in publishing English-language books about the arts, languages and cultures of Asia. The world has become a much smaller place today and Asia's economic and cultural influence has grown. Yet the need for meaningful dialogue and information about this diverse region has never been greater. Over the past seven decades, Tuttle has published thousands of books on subjects ranging from martial arts and paper crafts to language learning and literature — and our talented authors, illustrators, designers and photographers have won many prestigious awards. We welcome you to explore the wealth of information available on Asia at **www.tuttlepublishing.com**.